FOLK-TALES OF BENGAL

WARWICK GOBLE

FOLK-TALES OF BENGAL

LAL BEHARI DAY

WITH 32 ILLUSTRATIONS IN COLOUR
BY WARWICK GOBLE

ISBN : 978-93-5324-581-8 (HB)

First Published, London, 1912

Published, 2020

Published by

Facsimile Publisher
12 Pragati Market
Ashok Vihar, Ph-2
Delhi-110052
E-mail: books@facsimilepublisher.com

Printed at: G. Print Process, Delhi.

Folk-Tales of Bengal

Author: Lal Behari Day

FOLK-TALES OF BENGAL

BY THE

REV. LAL BEHARI DAY

AUTHOR OF 'BENGAL PEASANT LIFE,' ETC.

WITH 32 ILLUSTRATIONS IN COLOUR
BY WARWICK GOBLE

MACMILLAN AND CO., LIMITED
ST. MARTIN'S STREET, LONDON
1912

TO

RICHARD CARNAC TEMPLE

CAPTAIN, BENGAL STAFF CORPS

F.R.G.S., M.R.A.S., M.A.I., ETC.

WHO FIRST SUGGESTED TO THE WRITER

THE IDEA OF COLLECTING

THESE TALES

AND WHO IS DOING SO MUCH

IN THE CAUSE OF INDIAN FOLK-LORE

THIS LITTLE BOOK

IS INSCRIBED

PREFACE

In my *Peasant Life in Bengal* I make the peasant boy Govinda spend some hours every evening in listening to stories told by an old woman, who was called Sambhu's mother, and who was the best story-teller in the village. On reading that passage, Captain R. C. Temple, of the Bengal Staff Corps, son of the distinguished Indian administrator Sir Richard Temple, wrote to me to say how interesting it would be to get a collection of those unwritten stories which old women in India recite to little children in the evenings, and to ask whether I could not make such a collection. As I was no stranger to the *Mährchen* of the Brothers Grimm, to the *Norse Tales* so admirably told by Dasent, to Arnason's *Icelandic Stories* translated by Powell, to the *Highland Stories* done into English by Campbell, and to the fairy stories collected by other writers, and as I believed that the collection suggested would be a contribution, however slight, to that daily increasing literature of folk-lore and comparative mythology which, like comparative philosophy, proves that the swarthy and half-naked peasant on the banks of the Ganges is a cousin, albeit of the hundredth remove, to the fair-skinned and well-dressed Englishman on the banks of the Thames, I readily caught up the idea and cast about for materials. But where was an old story-telling woman to be got? I had myself, when a little boy, heard hundreds—it would be no exaggeration to say thousands—of fairy tales from that same old woman, Sambhu's mother—for she was no fictitious person; she actually lived in the flesh and bore that name; but I had nearly forgotten those stories, at any rate they had all got confused in my head, the tail of one story being joined to the head of another, and the head of a third to the tail of a fourth. How I wished that poor Sambhu's mother had been alive! But she had gone long, long ago, to that bourne from which no traveller returns, and her son Sambhu, too, had followed her thither. After a great deal of search I found my Gammer Grethel—though not half so old as the Frau Viehmännin of Hesse-Cassel—in the person of a Bengali Christian woman, who, when a little girl and living in her heathen home, had heard many stories from her old grandmother. She was a good story-teller, but her stock was not large; and after I had heard ten from her I had to look about for fresh sources. An old Brahman told me two stories; an old barber, three; an old servant of mine told me two; and the rest I heard from another old Brahman. None of my authorities knew English; they all told the stories in Bengali, and I translated them into English when I came home. I heard many more stories than those contained in the following pages; but I rejected a great many, as they appeared to me to contain spurious additions to the original stories which I had heard when a boy. I have reason to believe that the stories given in this book are a genuine sample of the old old stories told by old Bengali women from age to age through a hundred generations.

Sambhu's mother used always to end every one of her stories—and every orthodox Bengali story-teller does the same—with repeating the following formula :—

Thus my story endeth,
The Natiya-thorn withereth.
" *Why, O Natiya-thorn, dost wither ?*"
" *Why does thy cow on me browse ?*"
" *Why, O cow, dost thou browse ?*"
" *Why does thy neat-herd not tend me ?*"
" *Why, O neat-herd, dost not tend the cow ?*"
" *Why does thy daughter-in-law not give me rice?*"
" *Why, O daughter-in-law, dost not give rice ?*"
" *Why does my child cry ?*"
" *Why, O child, dost thou cry ?*"
" *Why does the ant bite me ?*"
" *Why, O ant, dost thou bite ?*"
Koot ! koot ! koot !

What these lines mean, why they are repeated at the end of every story, and what the connection is of the several parts to one another, I do not know. Perhaps the whole is a string of nonsense purposely put together to amuse little children.

LAL BEHARI DAY.

HOOGHLY COLLEGE,
February 27, 1883.

CONTENTS

CONTENTS

ILLUSTRATIONS

ILLUSTRATIONS

WARWICK GOBLE

"The Suo queen went to the door with a handful of rice."

I

LIFE'S SECRET

THERE was a king who had two queens, Duo and Suo.[1] Both of them were childless. One day a Faquir (mendicant) came to the palace-gate to ask for alms. The Suo queen went to the door with a handful of rice. The mendicant asked whether she had any children. On being answered in the negative, the holy mendicant refused to take alms, as the hands of a woman unblessed with child are regarded as ceremonially unclean. He offered her a drug for removing her barrenness, and she expressing her willingness to receive it, he gave it to her with the following directions :—"Take this nostrum, swallow it with the juice of the pomegranate flower ; if you do this, you will have a son in due time. The son will be exceedingly handsome, and his complexion will be of the colour of the pomegranate flower ; and you shall call him Dalim Kumar.[2] As enemies will try to take away the life of your son, I may as well tell

[1] Kings, in Bengali folk-tales, have invariably two queens—the elder is called *duo*, that is, not loved ; and the younger is called *suo*, that is, loved.

[2] *Dalim* or *dadimba* means a pomegranate, and *kumara* son.

you that the life of the boy will be bound up in the life of a big *boal* fish which is in your tank, in front of the palace. In the heart of the fish is a small box of wood, in the box is a necklace of gold, that necklace is the life of your son. Farewell."

In the course of a month or so it was whispered in the palace that the Suo queen had hopes of an heir. Great was the joy of the king. Visions of an heir to the throne, and of a never-ending succession of powerful monarchs perpetuating his dynasty to the latest generations, floated before his mind, and made him glad as he had never been in his life. The usual ceremonies performed on such occasions were celebrated with great pomp; and the subjects made loud demonstrations of their joy at the anticipation of so auspicious an event as the birth of a prince. In the fulness of time the Suo queen gave birth to a son of uncommon beauty. When the king the first time saw the face of the infant, his heart leaped with joy. The ceremony of the child's first rice was celebrated with extraordinary pomp, and the whole kingdom was filled with gladness.

In course of time Dalim Kumar grew up a fine boy. Of all sports he was most addicted to playing with pigeons. This brought him into frequent contact with his stepmother, the Duo queen, into whose apartments Dalim's pigeons had a trick of always flying. The first time the pigeons flew into her rooms, she readily gave them up to the owner; but the second time she gave them up with some reluctance. The fact is that the Duo queen, perceiving that Dalim's pigeons had this happy knack of flying into her apartments, wished to take advantage of it for the furtherance of her own selfish views. She naturally hated the child, as the king, since his birth, neglected her more than ever, and idolised the fortunate mother of Dalim. She had heard, it is not known how, that the holy mendicant that had given the famous pill to the Suo queen had also told her of a secret connected with the child's life. She had heard that the child's life was bound up with something—she did not know with what. She determined to extort that secret from the boy. Accordingly, the next time the pigeons flew into her rooms, she refused to give them up, addressing the child thus:—"I won't give the pigeons up unless you tell me one thing."

Dalim. What thing, mamma?

Duo. Nothing particular, my darling; I only want to know in what your life is.

Dalim. What is that, mamma? Where can my life be except in me?

Duo. No, child; that is not what I mean. A holy mendicant told your mother that your life is bound up with something. I wish to know what that thing is.

Dalim. I never heard of any such thing, mamma.

Duo. If you promise to inquire of your mother in what thing your life is, and if you tell me what your mother says, then I will let you have the pigeons, otherwise not.

Dalim. Very well, I'll inquire, and let you know. Now, please, give me my pigeons.

Duo. I'll give them on one condition more. Promise to me that you will not tell your mother that I want the information.

Dalim. I promise.

The Duo queen let go the pigeons, and Dalim, overjoyed to find again his beloved birds, forgot every syllable of the conversation he had had with his stepmother. The next day, however, the pigeons again flew into the Duo queen's rooms. Dalim went to his stepmother, who asked him for the required information. The boy promised to ask his mother that very day, and begged hard for the release of the pigeons. The pigeons were at last delivered. After play, Dalim went to his mother and said—"Mamma, please tell me in what my life is contained." "What do you mean, child?" asked the mother, astonished beyond measure at the child's extraordinary question. "Yes, mamma," rejoined the child, "I have heard that a holy mendicant told you that my life is contained in something. Tell me what that thing is." "My pet, my darling, my treasure, my golden moon, do not ask such an inauspicious question. Let the mouth of my enemies be covered with ashes, and let my Dalim live for ever," said the mother, earnestly. But the child insisted on being informed of the secret. He said he would not eat or drink anything unless the information were given him. The Suo queen, pressed by the importunity of her son, in an evil hour told the child the secret of his life. The next day the pigeons again, as fate would have it, flew into the Duo queen's rooms. Dalim went for them; the stepmother plied the boy with sugared words, and obtained the knowledge of the secret.

The Duo queen, on learning the secret of Dalim Kumar's life, lost no time in using it for the prosecution of her malicious design. She told her maid-servants to get for her some dried stalks of the hemp plant, which are very brittle, and which, when pressed upon, make a peculiar noise, not unlike the cracking of joints of bones in the human body. These hemp stalks she put under her bed, upon which she laid herself down and gave out that she was dangerously ill. The king, though he did not love her so well as his other queen, was in duty bound to visit her in her illness. The queen pretended that her bones were all cracking; and sure enough, when she tossed from one side of her bed to the other, the hemp stalks made the noise wanted. The king, believing that the Duo queen was seriously ill, ordered his best physician to attend her. With that physician the Duo queen was in collusion. The physician said to the king that for the queen's complaint there was but one remedy, which consisted in the outward application of something to be found inside a large *boal* fish which was in the tank before the palace. The king's fisherman was accordingly called and ordered to catch the *boal* in question. On the first throw of the net the fish was caught. It so happened that Dalim Kumar, along with other boys, was playing not far from the tank. The moment the *boal* fish was caught in the net, that moment Dalim felt unwell ; and when the fish was brought up to land, Dalim fell down on the ground, and made as if he was about to breathe his last. He was immediately taken into his mother's room, and the king was astonished on hearing of the sudden illness of his son and heir. The fish was by the order of the physician taken into the room of the Duo queen, and as it lay on the floor striking its fins on the ground, Dalim in his mother's room was given up for lost. When the fish was cut open, a casket was found in it ; and in the casket lay a necklace of gold. The moment the necklace was worn by the queen, that very moment Dalim died in his mother's room.

When the news of the death of his son and heir reached the king he was plunged into an ocean of grief, which was not lessened in any degree by the intelligence of the recovery of the Duo queen. He wept over his dead Dalim so bitterly that his courtiers were apprehensive of a permanent derangement of his mental powers. The king would not allow the dead body of his son to be either buried or burnt. He could not realise the fact of his son's death ; it was so entirely causeless and so terribly sudden. He ordered the dead body to be removed to one of his garden-houses in the suburbs of the city, and to be laid there in state. He ordered that all sorts of provisions should be stowed away in that house, as if the young prince needed them for his refection. Orders were issued that the house should be kept locked up day and night, and that no one should go into it except Dalim's most intimate friend, the son of the king's prime minister, who was intrusted with the key of the house, and who obtained the privilege of entering it once in twenty-four hours.

As, owing to her great loss, the Suo queen lived in retirement, the king gave up his nights entirely to the Duo queen. The latter, in order to allay suspicion, used to put aside the gold necklace at night ; and, as fate had ordained that Dalim should be in the state of death only during the time that the necklace was round the neck of the queen, he passed into the state of life whenever the necklace was laid aside. Accordingly Dalim revived every night, as the Duo queen every night put away the necklace, and died again the next morning when the queen put it on. When Dalim became reanimated at night he ate whatever food he liked, for of such there was a plentiful stock in the garden-house, walked about on the premises, and meditated on the singularity of his lot. Dalim's friend, who visited him only during the day, found him always lying a lifeless corpse ; but what struck him after some days was the singular fact that the body remained in the same state in which he saw it on the first day of his visit. There was no sign of putrefaction. Except that it was lifeless and pale, there were no symptoms of corruption—it was apparently quite fresh. Unable to account for so strange a phenomenon, he determined to watch the corpse more closely, and to visit it not only during the day but sometimes also at night. The first night that he paid his visit he was astounded to see his dead friend sauntering about in the garden. At first he thought the figure might be only the ghost of his friend, but on feeling him and otherwise examining him, he found the apparition to be veritable flesh and blood. Dalim related to his friend all the circumstances connected with his death; and they both concluded that he revived at nights only because the Duo queen put aside her necklace when the king visited her. As the life of the prince depended on the necklace, the two friends laid their heads together to devise if possible some plans by which they might get possession of it. Night after night they consulted together, but they could not think of any feasible scheme. At length the gods brought about the deliverance of Dalim Kumar in a wonderful manner.

Some years before the time of which we are speaking, the sister of Bidhata-Purusha[1] was delivered of a daughter. The anxious mother asked her brother what he had written on her child's forehead; to which Bidhata-Purusha replied that she should get married to a dead bridegroom. Maddened as she became with grief at the prospect of such a dreary destiny for her daughter,

[1] Bidhata-Purusha is the deity that predetermines all the events of the life of man or woman, and writes on the forehead of the child, on the sixth day of its birth, a brief *precis* of them.

WARWICK GOBLE

"The prince revived, and, walking about, saw a human figure near the gate."

she yet thought it useless to remonstrate with her brother, for she well knew that he never changed what he once wrote. As the child grew in years she became exceedingly beautiful, but the mother could not look upon her with pleasure in consequence of the portion allotted to her by her divine brother. When the girl came to marriageable age, the mother resolved to flee from the country with her, and thus avert her dreadful destiny. But the decrees of fate cannot thus be overruled. In the course of their wanderings the mother and daughter arrived at the gate of that very garden-house in which Dalim Kumar lay. It was evening. The girl said she was thirsty and wanted to drink water. The mother told her daughter to sit at the gate, while she went to search for drinking water in some neighbouring hut. In the meantime the girl through curiosity pushed the door of the garden-house, which opened of itself. She then went in and saw a beautiful palace, and was wishing to come out when the door shut itself of its own accord, so that she could not get out. As night came on the prince revived, and, walking about, saw a human figure near the gate. He went up to it, and found it was a girl of surpassing beauty. On being asked who she was, she told Dalim Kumar all the details of her little history,—how her uncle, the divine Bidhata-Purusha, wrote on her forehead at her birth that she should get married to a dead bridegroom, how her mother had no pleasure in her life at the prospect of so terrible a destiny, and how, therefore, on the approach of her womanhood, with a view to avert so dreadful a catastrophe, she had left her house with her and wandered in various places, how they came to the gate of the garden-house, and how her mother had now gone in search of drinking water for her. Dalim Kumar, hearing her simple and pathetic story, said, "I am the dead bridegroom, and you must get married to me, come with me to the house." "How can you be said to be a dead bridegroom when you are standing and speaking to me?" said the girl. "You will understand it afterwards," rejoined the prince, "come now and follow me." The girl followed the prince into the house. As she had been fasting the whole day the prince hospitably entertained her. As for the mother of the girl, the sister of the divine Bidhata-Purusha, she returned to the gate of the garden-house after it was dark, cried out for her daughter, and getting no answer, went away in search of her in the huts in the neighbourhood. It is said that after this she was not seen anywhere.

While the niece of the divine Bidhata-Purusha was partaking of the hospitality of Dalim Kumar, his friend as usual made his appearance. He was surprised not a little at the sight of the fair stranger; and his surprise became greater when he heard the story of the young lady from her own lips. It was forthwith resolved that very night to unite the young couple in the bonds of matrimony. As priests were out of the question, the hymeneal rites were performed *à la Gandharva*.[1] The friend of the bridegroom took leave of the newly-married couple and went away to his house. As the happy pair had spent the greater part of the night in wakefulness, it was long after sunrise that they awoke from their sleep ;—I should have said that the young wife woke from her sleep, for the prince had become a cold corpse, life having departed from him. The feelings of the young wife may be easily imagined. She shook her husband, imprinted warm kisses on his cold lips, but in vain. He was as lifeless as a marble statue. Stricken with horror, she smote her breast, struck her forehead with the palms of her hands, tore her hair and went about in the house and in the garden as if she had gone mad. Dalim's friend did not come into the house during the day, as he deemed it improper to pay a visit to her while her husband was lying dead. The day seemed to the poor girl as long as a year, but the longest day has its end, and when the shades of evening were descending upon the landscape, her dead husband was awakened into consciousness ; he rose up from his bed, embraced his disconsolate wife, ate, drank, and became merry. His friend made his appearance as usual, and the whole night was spent in gaiety and festivity. Amid this alternation of life and death did the prince and his lady spend some seven or eight years, during which time the princess presented her husband with two lovely boys who were the exact image of their father.

[1] There are eight forms of marriage spoken of in the Hindu Sastras, of which the Gandharva is one, consisting in the exchange of garlands.

It is superfluous to remark that the king, the two queens, and other members of the royal household did not know that Dalim Kumar was living, at any rate, was living at night. They all thought that he was long ago dead and his corpse burnt. But the heart of Dalim's wife was yearning after her mother-in-law, whom she had never seen. She conceived a plan by which she might be able not only to have a sight of her mother-in-law, but also to get hold of the Duo queen's necklace, on which her husband's life was dependent. With the consent of her husband and of his friend she disguised herself as a female barber. Like every female barber she took a bundle containing the following articles :—an iron instrument for paring nails, another iron instrument for scraping off the superfluous flesh of the soles of the feet, a piece of *jhama* or burnt brick for rubbing the soles of the feet with, and *alakta*[1] for painting the edges of the feet and toes with. Taking this bundle in her hand she stood at the gate of the king's palace with her two boys. She declared herself to be a barber, and expressed a desire to see the Suo queen, who readily gave her an interview. The queen was quite taken up with the two little boys, who, she declared, strongly reminded her of her darling Dalim Kumar. Tears fell profusely from her eyes at the recollection of her lost treasure ; but she of course had not the remotest idea that the two little boys were the sons of her own dear Dalim. She told the supposed barber that she did

[1] *Alakta* is leaves or flimsy paper saturated with lac.

not require her services, as, since the death of her son, she had given up all terrestrial vanities, and among others the practice of dyeing her feet red; but she added that, nevertheless, she would be glad now and then to see her and her two fine boys. The female barber, for so we must now call her, then went to the quarters of the Duo queen and offered her services. The queen allowed her to pare her nails, to scrape off the superfluous flesh of her feet, and to paint them with *alakta*, and was so pleased with her skill, and the sweetness of her disposition, that she ordered her to wait upon her periodically. The female barber noticed with no little concern the necklace round the queen's neck. The day of her second visit came on, and she instructed the elder of her two sons to set up a loud cry in the palace, and not to stop crying till he got into his hands the Duo queen's necklace. The female barber, accordingly, went again on the appointed day to the Duo queen's apartments. While she was engaged in painting the queen's feet, the elder boy set up a loud cry. On being asked the reason of the cry, the boy, as previously instructed, said that he wanted the queen's necklace. The queen said that it was impossible for her to part with that particular necklace, for it was the best and most valuable of all her jewels. To gratify the boy, however, she took it off her neck, and put it into the boy's hand. The boy stopped crying and held the necklace tight in his hand. As the female barber after she had done her work was about to go away, the queen wanted the necklace back. But the boy would not part with it. When his mother attempted to snatch it from him, he wept bitterly, and showed as if his heart would break. On which the female barber said—"Will your Majesty be gracious enough to let the boy take the necklace home with him? When he falls asleep after drinking his milk, which he is sure to do in the course of an hour, I will carefully bring it back to you." The queen, seeing that the boy would not allow it to be taken away from him, agreed to the proposal of the female barber, especially reflecting that Dalim, whose life depended on it, had long ago gone to the abodes of death.

Thus possessed of the treasure on which the life of her husband depended, the woman went with breathless haste to the garden-house and presented the necklace to Dalim, who had been restored to life. Their joy knew no bounds, and by the advice of their friend they determined the next day to go to the palace in state, and present themselves to the king and the Suo queen. Due preparations were made; an elephant, richly caparisoned, was brought for the prince Dalim Kumar, a pair of ponies for the two little boys, and a *chaturdala*[1] furnished with curtains of gold lace for the princess. Word was sent to the king and the Suo queen that the prince Dalim Kumar was not only alive, but that he was coming to visit his royal parents with his wife and sons. The king and Suo queen could hardly believe in the report, but being assured of

[1] A sort of open *Palki*, used generally for carrying the bridegroom and bride in marriage processions.

its truth they were entranced with joy; while the Duo queen, anticipating the disclosure of all her wiles, became overwhelmed with grief. The procession of Dalim Kumar, which was attended by a band of musicians, approached the palace-gate; and the king and Suo queen went out to receive their long-lost son. It is needless to say that their joy was intense. They fell on each other's neck and wept. Dalim then related all the circumstances connected with his death. The king, inflamed with rage, ordered the Duo queen into his presence. A large hole, as deep as the height of a man, was dug in the ground. The Duo queen was put into it in a standing posture. Prickly thorn was heaped around her up to the crown of her head; and in this manner she was buried alive.

Thus my story endeth,
The Natiya-thorn withereth;
"*Why, O Natiya-thorn, dost wither?*"
"*Why does thy cow on me browse?*"
"*Why, O cow, dost thou browse?*"
"*Why does thy neat-herd not tend me?*"
"*Why, O neat-herd, dost not tend the cow?*"
"*Why does thy daughter-in-law not give me rice?*"
"*Why, O daughter-in-law, dost not give rice?*"
"*Why does my child cry?*"
"*Why, O child, dost thou cry?*"
"*Why does the ant bite me?*"
"*Why, O ant, dost thou bite?*"
Koot! koot! koot!

II

PHAKIR CHAND

THERE was a king's son, and there was a minister's son. They loved each other dearly; they sat together, they stood up together, they walked together, they ate together, they slept together, they got up together. In this way they spent many years in each other's company, till they both felt a desire to see foreign lands. So one day they set out on their journey. Though very rich, the one being the son of a king and the other the son of his chief minister, they did not take any servants with them; they went by themselves on horseback. The horses were beautiful to look at; they were *pakshirajes*, or kings of birds. The king's son and the minister's son rode together many days. They passed through extensive plains covered with paddy; through cities, towns, and villages; through waterless, treeless deserts; through dense forests which were the abode of the tiger and the bear. One evening they were overtaken by night in a region where human habitations were not seen; and as it was getting darker and darker, they dismounted beneath a lofty tree, tied their horses to its trunk, and, climbing up, sat on its branches covered with thick foliage. The tree grew near a large tank, the water of which was as clear as the eye of a crow. The king's son and the minister's son made themselves as comfortable as they could on the tree, being determined to spend on its branches the livelong night. They sometimes chatted together in whispers on account of the lonely terrors of the region; they sometimes sat demurely silent for some minutes; and anon they were falling into a doze, when their attention was arrested by a terrible sight.

A sound like the rush of many waters was heard from the middle of the tank. A huge serpent was seen leaping up from under the water with its hood of enormous size. It "lay floating many a rood"; then it swam ashore, and went about hissing. But what most of all attracted the attention of the king's son and the minister's son was a brilliant *manikya* (jewel) on the crested hood of the serpent. It shone like a thousand diamonds. It lit up the tank, its embankments, and the objects round about. The serpent doffed the jewel from its crest and threw it on the ground, and then it went about hissing in search of food. The two friends sitting on the tree greatly admired the wonderful brilliant, shedding ineffable lustre on everything around. They had never before seen anything like it; they had only heard of it as equalling the treasures of seven kings. Their admiration, however, was soon changed into sorrow and fear; for the serpent came hissing to the foot of the tree on the branches of which they were seated, and swallowed up, one by one, the horses tied to the trunk. They feared that they themselves would be the next victims, when, to their infinite relief, the gigantic cobra turned away from the tree, and went about roaming to a great distance. The minister's son, seeing this, bethought himself of taking possession of the lustrous stone. He had heard that the only way to hide the brilliant light of the jewel was to cover it with cow-dung or horse-dung, a quantity of which latter article he perceived lying at the foot of the tree. He came down from the tree softly, picked up the horse-dung, threw it upon the precious stone, and again climbed into the tree. The serpent, not perceiving the light of its head-jewel, rushed with great fury to the spot where it had been left. Its hissings, groans, and convulsions were terrible. It went round and round the jewel covered with horse-dung, and then breathed its last. Early next morning the king's son and the minister's son alighted from the tree, and went to the spot where the crest-jewel was. The mighty serpent lay there perfectly lifeless. The minister's son took up in his hand the jewel covered with horse-dung; and both of them went to the tank to wash it. When all the horse-dung had been washed off, the jewel shone as brilliantly as before. It lit up the entire bed of the tank, and exposed to their view the innumerable fishes swimming about in the waters. But what was their astonishment when they saw, by the light of the jewel, in the bottom of the tank, the lofty walls of what seemed a magnificent palace. The venturesome son of the minister proposed to the prince that they should dive into the waters and get at the palace below. They both dived into the waters—the jewel being in the hand of the minister's son—and in a moment stood at the gate of the palace. The gate was open. They saw no being, human or superhuman. They went inside the gate, and saw a beautiful garden laid out on the ample grounds round about the house which was in the centre. The king's son and the minister's son had never seen such a profusion of flowers. The rose with its many varieties, the jessamine, the *bel*, the *mallika*, the *king of smells*, the lily of the valley, the *Champaka*, and a thousand other sorts of sweet-scented flowers were there. And of each of these flowers there seemed to be a large number. Here were a hundred rose-bushes, there many acres covered with the delicious jessamine, while yonder were extensive plantations of all sorts of flowers. As all the plants were begemmed with flowers, and as the flowers were in full bloom, the air was loaded with rich perfume. It was a wilderness of sweets. Through this paradise of perfumery they proceeded towards the house, which was surrounded by banks of lofty trees. They stood at the door of the house. It was a fairy palace. The walls were of burnished gold, and here and there shone diamonds of dazzling hue which were stuck into the walls. They did not meet with any beings, human or other. They went inside, which was richly furnished. They went from room to room, but they did not see any one. It seemed to be a deserted house. At last, however, they found in one room a young lady lying down, apparently in sleep, on a bed of golden framework. She was of exquisite beauty; her complexion was a mixture of red and white; and her age was apparently about sixteen. The king's son and the minister's son gazed upon her with rapture; but they had not stood long when this young lady of superb beauty opened her eyes, which seemed like those of a gazelle. On seeing the strangers she said: "How have you come here, ye unfortunate men? Begone, begone! This is the abode of a mighty serpent, which has devoured my father, my mother, my brothers, and all my relatives; I am the only one of my family that he has spared. Flee for your lives, or else the serpent will put you both in its capacious maw." The minister's son told the princess how the serpent had breathed its last; how he and his friend had got possession of its head-jewel, and by its light had come to her palace. She thanked the strangers for delivering her from the infernal serpent, and begged of them to live in the house, and never to desert her. The king's son and the minister's son gladly accepted the invitation. The king's son, smitten with the charms of the peerless princess, married her after a short time; and as there was no priest there, the hymeneal knot was tied by a simple exchange of garlands of flowers.

The king's son became inexpressibly happy in the company of the princess, who was as amiable in her disposition as she was beautiful in her person ; and though the wife of the minister's son was living in the upper world, he too participated in his friend's happiness. Time thus passed merrily, when the king's son bethought himself of returning to his native country ; and as it was fit that he should go with his princess in due pomp, it was determined that the minister's son should first ascend from the subaqueous regions, go to the king, and bring with him attendants, horses, and elephants for the happy pair. The snake-jewel was therefore had in requisition. The prince, with the jewel in hand, accompanied the minister's son to the upper world, and bidding adieu to his friend returned to his lovely wife in the enchanted palace. Before leaving, the minister's son appointed the day and the hour when he would stand on the high embankments of the tank with horses, elephants, and attendants, and wait upon the prince and the princess, who were to join him in the upper world by means of the jewel.

Leaving the minister's son to wend his way to his country and to make preparations for the return of his king's son, let us see how the happy couple in the subterranean palace were passing their time. One day, while the prince was sleeping after his noonday meal, the princess, who had never seen the upper regions, felt the desire of visiting them, and the rather as the snake-jewel, which alone could give her safe conduct through the waters, was at that moment shedding its bright effulgence in the room. She took up the jewel in her hand, left the palace, and successfully reached the upper world. No mortal caught her sight. She sat on the flight of steps with which the tank was furnished for the convenience of bathers, scrubbed her body, washed her hair, disported in the waters, walked about on the water's edge, admired all the scenery around, and returned to her palace, where she found her husband still locked in the embrace of sleep. When the prince woke up, she did not tell him a word about her adventure. The following day at the same hour, when her husband was asleep, she paid a second visit to the upper world, and went back unnoticed by mortal man. As success made her bold, she repeated her adventure a third time. It so chanced that on that day the son of the Rajah, in whose territories the tank was situated, was out on a hunting excursion, and had pitched his tent not far from the place. While his attendants were engaged in cooking their noon-day meal, the Rajah's son sauntered about on the embankments of the tank, near which an old woman was gathering sticks and dried branches of trees for purposes of fuel. It was while the Rajah's son and the old woman were near the tank that the princess paid her third visit to the upper world. She rose up from the waters, gazed around, and seeing a man and a woman on the banks again went down. The Rajah's son caught a momentary glimpse of the princess, and so did the old woman gathering sticks. The Rajah's son stood gazing on the waters. He had never seen such a beauty.

"She took up the jewel in her hand, left the palace, and successfully reached the upper world."

WARWICK GOBLE

She seemed to him to be one of those *deva-kanyas*, heavenly goddesses, of whom he had read in old books, and who are said now and then to favour the lower world with their visits, which, like angel visits, are "few and far between." The unearthly beauty of the princess, though he had seen her only for a moment, made a deep impression on his heart, and distracted his mind. He stood there like a statue, for hours, gazing on the waters, in the hope of seeing the lovely figure again. But in vain. The princess did not appear again. The Rajah's son became mad with love. He kept muttering—"Now here, now gone! Now here, now gone!" He would not leave the place till he was forcibly removed by the attendants who had now come to him. He was taken to his father's palace in a state of hopeless insanity. He spoke to nobody; he always sobbed heavily; and the only words which proceeded out of his mouth—and he was muttering them every minute—were, "Now here, now gone! Now here, now gone!" The Rajah's grief may well be conceived. He could not imagine what should have deranged his son's mind. The words, "Now here, now gone," which ever and anon issued from his son's lips, were a mystery to him; he could not unravel their meaning; neither could the attendants throw any light on the subject. The best physicians of the country were consulted, but to no effect. The sons of Æsculapius could not ascertain the cause of the madness, far less could they cure it. To the many inquiries of the physicians, the only reply made by the Rajah's son was the stereotyped words—"Now here, now gone! Now here, now gone!"

The Rajah, distracted with grief on account of the obscuration of his son's intellects, caused a proclamation to be made in the capital by beat of drum, to the effect that, if any person could explain the cause of his son's madness and cure it, such a person would be rewarded with the hand of the Rajah's daughter, and with the possession of half his kingdom. The drum was beaten round most parts of the city, but no one touched it, as no one knew the cause of the madness of the Rajah's son. At last an old woman touched the drum, and declared that she would not only discover the cause of the madness, but cure it. This woman, who was the identical woman that was gathering sticks near the tank at the time the Rajah's son lost his reason, had a crack-brained son of the name of Phakir Chand, and was in consequence called Phakir's mother, or more familiarly Phakre's mother. When the woman was brought before the Rajah, the following conversation took place:—

Rajah. You are the woman that touched the drum.—You know the cause of my son's madness?

Phakir's Mother. Yes, O incarnation of justice! I know the cause, but I will not mention it till I have cured your son.

Rajah. How can I believe that you are able to cure my son, when the best physicians of the land have failed?

Phakir's Mother. You need not now believe, my lord, till I have performed the cure. Many an old woman knows secrets with which wise men are unacquainted.

Rajah. Very well, let me see what you can do. In what time will you perform the cure ?

Phakir's Mother. It is impossible to fix the time at present ; but I will begin work immediately with your lordship's assistance.

Rajah. What help do you require from me ?

Phakir's Mother. Your lordship will please order a hut to be raised on the embankment of the tank where your son first caught the disease. I mean to live in that hut for a few days. And your lordship will also please order some of your servants to be in attendance at a distance of about a hundred yards from the hut, so that they might be within call.

Rajah. Very well ; I will order that to be immediately done. Do you want anything else ?

Phakir's Mother. Nothing else, my lord, in the way of preparations. But it is as well to remind your lordship of the conditions on which I undertake the cure. Your lordship has promised to give to the performer of the cure the hand of your daughter and half your kingdom. As I am a woman and cannot marry your daughter, I beg that, in case I perform the cure, my son Phakir Chand may marry your daughter and take possession of half your kingdom.

Rajah. Agreed, agreed.

A temporary hut was in a few hours erected

on the embankment of the tank, and Phakir's mother took up her abode in it. An outpost was also erected at some distance for servants in attendance who might be required to give help to the woman. Strict orders were given by Phakir's mother that no human being should go near the tank excepting herself. Let us leave Phakir's mother keeping watch at the tank, and hasten down into the subterranean palace to see what the prince and the princess are about. After the mishap which had occurred on her last visit to the upper world, the princess had given up the idea of a fourth visit. But women generally have greater curiosity than men; and the princess of the underground palace was no exception to the general rule. One day, while her husband was asleep as usual after his noonday meal, she rushed out of the palace with the snake-jewel in her hand, and came to the upper world. The moment the upheaval of the waters in the middle of the tank took place, Phakir's mother, who was on the alert, concealed herself in the hut and began looking through the chinks of the matted wall. The princess, seeing no mortal near, came to the bank, and sitting there began to scrub her body. Phakir's mother showed herself outside the hut, and addressing the princess, said in a winning tone —"Come, my child, thou queen of beauty, come to me, and I will help you to bathe." So saying, she approached the princess, who, seeing that it was only a woman, made no resistance. The old woman, while in the act of washing the hair of the princess, noticed the bright jewel in her hand, and said—" Put the jewel here till you are bathed." In a moment the jewel was in the possession of Phakir's mother, who wrapped it up in the cloth that was round her waist. Knowing the princess to be unable to escape, she gave the signal to the attendants in waiting, who rushed to the tank and made the princess a captive.

Great were the rejoicings of the people when the tidings reached the city that Phakir's mother had captured a water-nymph from the nether regions. The whole city came to see the "daughter of the immortals," as they called the princess. When she was brought to the palace and confronted with the Rajah's son of obscured intellect, the latter said with a shout of exultation—" I have found! I have found!" The cloud which had settled on his brain was dissipated in a moment. The eyes, erewhile vacant and lustreless, now glowed with the fire of intelligence; his tongue, of which he had almost lost the use—the only words which he used to utter being, " Now here, now gone!"—was now relaxed: in a word, he was restored to his senses. The joy of the Rajah knew no bounds. There was great festivity in the city; and the people who showered benedictions on the head of Phakir Chand's mother, expected the speedy celebration of the marriage of the Rajah's son with the beauty of the nether world. The princess, however, told the Rajah, through Phakir's mother, that she had made a vow to the effect that she would not, for one whole year, look at the face of another man than that of her husband who was dwelling beneath the waters, and that therefore the marriage could not be performed during that period. Though the Rajah's son was somewhat disappointed, he readily agreed to the delay, believing, agreeably to the proverb, that delay would greatly enhance the sweetness of those pleasures which were in store for him.

It is scarcely necessary to say that the princess spent her days and her nights in sorrowing and sighing. She lamented that idle curiosity which had led her to come to the upper world, leaving her husband below. When she recollected that her husband was all alone below the waters she wept bitter tears. She wished she could run away. But that was impossible, as she was immured within walls, and there were walls within walls. Besides, if she could get out of the palace and of the city, of what avail would it be? She could not gain her husband, as the serpent jewel was not in her possession. The ladies of the palace and Phakir's mother tried to divert her mind, but in vain. She took pleasure in nothing; she would hardly speak to any one; she wept day and night. The year of her vow was drawing to a close, and yet she was disconsolate. The marriage, however, must be celebrated. The Rajah consulted the astrologers, and the day and the hour in which the nuptial knot was to be tied were fixed. Great preparations were made. The confectioners of the city busied themselves day and night in preparing sweetmeats; milkmen took contracts for supplying the palace with tanks of curds; gunpowder was being manufactured for a grand display of fireworks; bands of musicians were placed on sheds erected over the palace gate, who ever and anon sent forth many "a bout of linked sweetness"; and the whole city assumed an air of mirth and festivity.

It is time we should think of the minister's son, who, leaving his friend in the subterranean palace, had gone to his country to bring horses, elephants, and attendants for the return of the king's son and his lovely princess with due pomp. The preparations took him many months; and when everything was ready he started on his journey, accompanied by a long train of elephants, horses, and attendants. He reached the tank two or three days before the appointed day. Tents were pitched in the mango-topes adjoining the tank for the accommodation of men and cattle; and the minister's son always kept his eyes fixed on the tank. The sun of the appointed day sank below the horizon; but the prince and the princess dwelling beneath the waters made no sign. He waited two or three days longer; still the prince did not make his appearance. What could have happened to his friend and his beautiful wife? Were they dead? Had another serpent, possibly the mate of the one that had died, beaten the prince and the princess to death? Had they somehow lost the serpent-jewel? Or had they been captured when they were once on a visit to the upper world? Such were the reflections of the minister's son. He was overwhelmed with grief. Ever since he had come to the tank he had heard at regular intervals the sound of music coming from the city which was not distant. He inquired of passers-by what that music meant. He was told that the Rajah's son was about to be married to some wonderful young lady, who had come out of the waters of that very tank on the bank of which he was now seated, and that the marriage ceremony was to be performed on the day following the next. The minister's son immediately concluded that the wonderful young lady of the lake that was to be married was none other than the wife of his friend, the king's son. He resolved therefore to go into the city to learn the details of the affair, and try if possible to rescue the princess. He told the attendants to go home, taking with them the elephants and the horses; and he himself went to the city, and took up his abode in the house of a Brahman.

After he had rested and taken his dinner, the minister's son asked the Brahman what the meaning was of the music that was heard in the city at regular intervals. The Brahman asked, "From what part of the world have you come that you have not heard of the wonderful circumstance that a young lady of heavenly beauty rose out of the waters of a tank in the suburbs, and that she is going to be married the day after to-morrow to the son of our Rajah?"

Minister's Son. No, I have heard nothing. I have come from a distant country whither the story has not reached. Will you kindly tell me the particulars?

Brahman. The Rajah's son went out a-hunting about this time last year. He pitched his tents close to a tank in the suburbs. One day, while the Rajah's son was walking near the tank, he saw a young woman, or rather goddess, of uncommon beauty rise from the waters of the tank. She gazed about for a minute or two and disappeared. The Rajah's son, however, who had seen her, was so struck with her heavenly beauty that he became desperately enamoured of her. Indeed, so intense was his passion, that his reason gave way; and he was carried home hopelessly mad. The only words he uttered day and night were—"Now here, now gone!" The Rajah sent for all the best physicians of the country for restoring his son to his reason; but the physicians were powerless. At last he caused a proclamation to be made by beat of drum to the effect that if any one could cure the Rajah's son, he should be the Rajah's son-in-law and the owner of half his kingdom. An old woman, who went by the name of Phakir's mother, took hold of the drum, and declared her ability to cure the Rajah's son. On the tank where the princess had appeared was raised for Phakir's mother a hut in which she took up her abode; and not far from her hut another hut was erected for the accommodation of attendants who might be required to help her. It seems the goddess rose from the waters; Phakir's mother seized her with the help of the attendants, and carried her in a *palki* to the palace. At the sight of her the Rajah's son was restored to his senses; and the marriage would have been celebrated at that time but for a vow which the goddess had made that she would not look at the face of any male person till the lapse of a year. The year of the vow is now over; and the music which you have heard is from the gate of the Rajah's palace. This, in brief, is the story.

Minister's Son. A truly wonderful story! And has Phakir's mother, or rather Phakir Chand himself, been rewarded with the hand of the Rajah's daughter and with the possession of half the kingdom?

Brahman. No, not yet. Phakir has not been got hold of. He is a half-witted lad, or rather quite mad. He has been away for more than a year from his home, and no one knows where he is. That is his manner; he stays away for a long time, suddenly comes home, and again disappears. I believe his mother expects him soon.

Minister's Son. What like is he? and what does he do when he returns home?

Brahman. Why, he is about your height, though he is somewhat younger than you. He puts on a small piece of cloth round his waist, rubs his body with ashes, takes the branch of a tree in his hand, and, at the door of the hut in which his mother lives, dances to the tune of *dhoop! dhoop! dhoop!* His articulation is very indistinct; and when his mother says—"Phakir! stay with me for some days," he invariably answers in his usual unintelligible manner, "No, I won't remain, I won't remain." And when he wishes to give an affirmative answer, he says, "Hoom," which means "Yes."

The above conversation with the Brahman poured a flood of light into the mind of the minister's son. He saw how matters stood. He perceived that the princess of the subterranean palace must have alone ventured out into the tank by means of the snake-jewel; that she must have been captured alone without the king's son; that the snake-jewel must be in the possession of Phakir's mother; and that his friend, the king's son, must be alone below the waters without any means of escape. The desolate and apparently hopeless state of his friend filled him with unutterable grief. He was in deep musings during most part of the night. Is it impossible, thought he, to rescue the king's son from the nether regions? What if, by some means or other, I contrive to get the jewel from the old woman? And can I not do it by personating Phakir Chand himself, who is expected by his mother shortly? And possibly by the same means I may be able to rescue the princess from the Rajah's palace. He resolved to act the *rôle* of Phakir Chand the following day. In the morning he left the Brahman's house, went to the outskirts of the city, divested himself of his usual clothing, put round his waist a short and narrow piece of cloth which scarcely reached his knee-joints, rubbed his body well with ashes, took in his hand a twig which he broke off a tree, and thus accoutred, presented himself before the door of the hut of Phakir's mother. He commenced operations by dancing, in a most violent manner, to the tune of *dhoop! dhoop! dhoop!* The dancing attracted the notice of the old woman, who, supposing that her son had come, said—"My son Phakir, are you come? Come, my darling; the gods have at last become propitious to us." The supposed Phakir Chand uttered the monosyllable "hoom," and went on dancing in a still more violent manner than before, waving the twig in his hand. "This time you must not go away," said the old woman, "you must remain with me." "No, I won't remain, I won't remain," said the minister's son. "Remain with me, and I'll get you married to the Rajah's daughter. Will you marry, Phakir Chand?" The minister's son replied—"Hoom, hoom," and danced on like a madman. "Will you come with me to the Rajah's house? I'll show you a princess of uncommon beauty who has risen from the waters." "Hoom, hoom," was the answer that issued from his lips, while his feet tripped it violently to the sound of *dhoop! dhoop!* "Do you wish to see a *manik*, Phakir, the crest jewel of the serpent, the treasure of seven kings?" "Hoom, hoom," was the reply. The old woman brought out of the hut the snake-jewel, and put it into the hand of her supposed son. The minister's son took it, and carefully wrapped it up in the piece of cloth round his waist. Phakir's mother, delighted beyond measure at the opportune appearance of her son, went to the Rajah's house, partly to announce to the Rajah the news of Phakir's appearance, and partly to show Phakir the princess of the waters. The supposed Phakir and his mother found ready access to the Rajah's palace, for the old woman had, since the capture of the princess, become the most important person in the kingdom. She took him into the room where the princess was, and introduced him to her. It is superfluous to remark that the princess was by no means pleased with the company of a madcap, who was in a state of semi-nudity, whose body was rubbed with ashes, and who was ever and anon dancing in a wild manner. At sunset the old woman proposed to her son that they should leave the palace and go to their own house. But the supposed Phakir Chand refused to comply with the request; he said he would stay there that night. His mother tried to persuade him to return with her, but he persisted in his determination. He said he would remain with the princess. Phakir's mother therefore went away, after giving instructions to the guards and attendants to take care of her son.

When all in the palace had retired to rest, the supposed Phakir, coming towards the princess, said in his own usual voice—"Princess! do you not recognise me? I am the minister's son, the friend of your princely husband." The princess, astonished at the announcement, said—"Who? The minister's son? Oh, my husband's best friend, do rescue me from this terrible captivity, from this worse than death. O fate! it is by my own fault that I am reduced to this wretched state. Oh, rescue me, rescue me, thou best of friends!" She then burst into tears. The minister's son said, "Do not be disconsolate. I will try my best to rescue you this very night; only you must do whatever I tell you." "I will do anything you tell me, minister's son; anything you tell me." After this the supposed Phakir left the room, and passed through the courtyard of the palace. Some of the guards challenged him, to whom he replied, "Hoom, hoom; I will just go out for a minute and again come in presently." They understood that it was the madcap Phakir. True to his word he did come back shortly, and went to the princess. An hour afterwards he again went out and was again challenged, on which he made the same reply as at the first time. The guards who challenged him began to mutter between their teeth—"This madcap of a Phakir will, we suppose, go out and come in all night. Let the fellow alone; let him do what he likes. Who can be sitting up all night for him?" The minister's son was going out and coming in with the view of accustoming the guards to his constant egress and ingress, and also of watching for a favourable opportunity to escape with the princess. About three o'clock in the morning the minister's son again passed through the courtyard, but this time no one challenged him, as all the guards had fallen asleep. Overjoyed at the auspicious circumstance, he went to the princess. "Now, princess, is the time for escape. The guards are all asleep.

Mount on my back, and tie the locks of your hair round my neck, and keep tight hold of me." The princess did as she was told. He passed unchallenged through the courtyard with the lovely burden on his back, passed out of the gate of the palace—no one challenging him, passed on to the outskirts of the city, and reached the tank from which the princess had risen. The princess stood on her legs, rejoicing at her escape, and at the same time trembling. The minister's son untied the snake-jewel from his waist-cloth, and descending into the waters, both he and she found their way to the subterranean palace. The reception which the prince in the subaqueous palace gave to his wife and his friend may be easily imagined. He had nearly died of grief; but now he suffered a resurrection. The three were now mad with joy. During the three days that they remained in the palace they again and again told the story of the egress of the princess into the upper world, of her seizure, of her captivity in the palace, of the preparations for marriage, of the old woman, of the minister's son personating Phakir Chand, and of the successful deliverance. It is unnecessary to add that the prince and the princess expressed their gratitude to the minister's son in the warmest terms, declared him to be their best and greatest friend, and vowed to abide always, till the day of their death, by his advice, and to follow his counsel.

Being resolved to return to their native country, the king's son, the minister's son, and the princess left the subterranean palace, and, lighted in the passage by the snake-jewel, made their way good to the upper world. As they had neither elephants nor horses, they were under the necessity of travelling on foot; and though this mode of travelling was troublesome to both the king's son and the minister's son, as they were bred in the lap of luxury, it was infinitely more troublesome to the princess, as the stones of the rough road

"*Wounded the invisible*
Palms of her tender feet where'er they fell."

When her feet became very sore, the king's son sometimes took her up on his broad shoulders, on which she sat astride; but the load, however lovely, was too heavy to be carried any great distance. She therefore, for the most part, travelled on foot.

One evening they bivouacked beneath a tree, as no human habitations were visible. The minister's son said to the prince and princess, "Both of you go to sleep, and I will keep watch in order to prevent any danger." The royal couple were soon locked in the arms of sleep. The faithful son of the minister did not sleep, but sat up watching. It so happened that on that tree swung the nest of the two immortal birds, Bihangama and Bihangami, who were not only endowed with the power of human speech, but who could see into the future. To the no little astonishment of the minister's son the two prophetical birds joined in the following conversation:—

Bihangama. The minister's son has already risked his own life for the safety of his friend, the king's son ; but he will find it difficult to save the prince at last.

Bihangami. Why so ?

Bihangama. Many dangers await the king's son. The prince's father, when he hears of the approach of his son, will send for him an elephant, some horses, and attendants. When the king's son rides on the elephant he will fall down and die.

Bihangami. But suppose some one prevents the king's son from riding on the elephant, and makes him ride on horseback, will he not in that case be saved ?

Bihangama. Yes, he will in that case escape that danger, but a fresh danger awaits him. When the king's son is in sight of his father's palace, and when he is in the act of passing through its lion-gate, the lion-gate will fall upon him and crush him to death.

Bihangami. But suppose some one destroys the lion-gate before the king's son goes up to it ; will not the king's son in that case be saved ?

Bihangama. Yes, in that case he will escape that particular danger ; but a fresh danger awaits him. When the king's son reaches the palace and sits at a feast prepared for him, and when he takes into his mouth the head of a fish cooked for him, the head of the fish will stick in his throat and choke him to death.

Bihangami. But suppose some one sitting at the feast snatches the head of the fish from the prince's plate, and thus prevents him from putting it into his mouth, will not the king's son in that case be saved ?

Bihangama. Yes, in that case he will escape that particular danger ; but a fresh danger awaits him. When the prince and princess after dinner retire into their sleeping apartment, and they lie together in bed, a terrible cobra will come into the room and bite the king's son to death.

Bihangami. But suppose some one lying in wait in the room cut the snake into pieces, will not the king's son in that case be saved ?

Bihangama. Yes, in that case the life of the king's son will be saved ; but if the man who kills the snake repeats to the king's son the conversation between you and me, that man will be turned into a marble statue.

Bihangami. But is there no means of restoring the marble statue to life ?

Bihangama. Yes, the marble statue may be restored to life if it is washed with the life-blood of the infant which the princess will give birth to, immediately after it is ushered into the world.

The conversation of the prophetical birds had extended thus far when the crows began to caw, the east put on a reddish hue, and the travellers beneath the tree bestirred themselves. The conversation stopped, but the minister's son had heard it all.

The prince, the princess, and the minister's son pursued their journey in the morning ; but they had not walked many hours when they met a procession consisting of an elephant, a horse, a *palki*, and a large number of attendants. These animals and men had been sent by the king, who had heard that his son, together with his newly married wife and his friend the minister's son, were not far from the capital on their journey homewards. The elephant, which was richly caparisoned, was intended for the prince ; the *palki*, the framework of which was silver and was gaudily adorned, was meant for the princess ; and the horse for the minister's son. As the prince was about to mount on the elephant, the minister's son went up to him and said—"Allow me to ride on the elephant, and you please ride on horseback." The prince was not a little surprised at the coolness of the proposal. He thought his friend was presuming too much on the services he had rendered ; he was therefore nettled, but remembering that his friend had saved both him and his wife, he said nothing, but quietly mounted the horse, though his mind became somewhat alienated from him. The procession started, and after some time came in sight of the palace, the lion-gate of which had been gaily adorned for the reception of the prince and the princess. The minister's son told the prince that the lion-gate should be broken down before the prince could enter the palace. The prince was astounded at the proposal, especially as the minister's son gave no reasons for so extraordinary a request. His mind became still more estranged from him ; but in consideration of the services the minister's son had rendered, his request was complied with, and the beautiful lion-gate, with its gay decorations, was broken down.

The party now went into the palace, where the king gave a warm reception to his son, to his daughter-in-law, and to the minister's son. When the story of their adventures was related, the king and his courtiers expressed great astonishment, and they all with one voice extolled the sagacity, prudence, and devotedness of the minister's son. The ladies of the palace were struck with the extraordinary beauty of the new-comer ; her complexion was milk and vermilion mixed together ; her neck was like that of a swan ; her eyes were like those of a gazelle ; her lips were as red as the berry *bimba* ; her cheeks were lovely ; her nose was straight and high ; her hair reached her ankles ; her walk was as graceful as that of a young elephant—such were the terms in which the connoisseurs of beauty praised the princess whom destiny had brought into the midst of them. They sat around her and put her a thousand questions regarding her parents, regarding the subterranean palace in which she formerly lived, and the serpent which had killed all her relatives. It was now time that the new arrivals should have their dinner. The dinner was served up in dishes of gold. All sorts of delicacies were there, amongst which the most conspicuous was the large head of a *rohita* fish placed in a golden cup near the prince's plate. While they were eating, the minister's son suddenly snatched the head of the fish from the prince's plate, and said, "Let me,

"He rushed out of his hiding-place and killed the serpent."

prince, eat this *rohita's* head." The king's son was quite indignant. He said nothing, however. The minister's son perceived that his friend was in a terrible rage; but he could not help it, as his conduct, however strange, was necessary to the safety of his friend's life; neither could he clear himself by stating the reason of his behaviour, as in that case he himself would be transformed into a marble statue. The dinner over, the minister's son expressed his desire to go to his own house. At other times the king's son would not allow his friend to go away in that fashion; but being shocked at his strange conduct, he readily agreed to the proposal. The minister's son, however, had not the slightest notion of going to his own house; he was resolved to avert the last peril that was to threaten the life of his friend. Accordingly, with a sword in his hand, he stealthily entered the room in which the prince and the princess were to sleep that night, and ensconced himself under the bedstead, which was furnished with mattresses of down and canopied with mosquito curtains of the richest silk and gold lace. Soon after dinner the prince and princess came into the bedroom, and undressing themselves went to bed. At midnight, while the royal couple were asleep, the minister's son perceived a snake of gigantic size enter the room through one of the water-passages, and climb up the tester-frame of the bed. He rushed out of his hiding-place, killed the serpent, cut it up in pieces, and put the pieces in the dish for holding betel-leaves and spices. It so happened, however, that as the minister's son was cutting the serpent into pieces, a drop of blood fell on the breast of the princess, and the rather as the mosquito curtains had not been let down. Thinking that the drop of blood might injure the fair princess, he resolved to lick it up. But as he regarded it as a great sin to look upon a young woman lying asleep half naked, he blindfolded himself with seven-fold cloth, and licked up the drop of blood. But while he was in the act of licking it, the princess awoke and screamed, and her scream roused her husband lying beside her. The prince seeing the minister's son, who he thought had gone away to his own house, bending over the body of his wife, fell into a great rage, and would have got up and killed him, had not the minister's son besought him to restrain his anger, adding—"Friend, I have done this only in order to save your life." "I do not understand what you mean," said the prince ; "ever since we came out of the subterranean palace you have been behaving in a most extraordinary way. In the first place, you prevented me from getting upon the richly caparisoned elephant, though my father, the king, had purposely sent it for me. I thought, however, that a sense of the services you had rendered to me had made you exceedingly vain ; I therefore let the matter pass, and mounted the horse. In the second place, you insisted on the destruction of the fine lion-gate, which my father had adorned with gay decorations ; and I let that matter also pass. Then, again, at dinner you snatched away, in a most shameful manner, the *rohita's* head which was on my plate, and devoured it yourself, thinking, no doubt, that you were entitled to higher honours than I. You then pretended that you were going home, for which I was not at all sorry, as you had made yourself very disagreeable to me. And now you are actually in my bedroom, bending over the naked bosom of my wife. You must have had some evil design ; and you pretend that you have done this to save my life. I fancy it was not for saving my life, but for destroying my wife's chastity." "Oh, do not harbour such thoughts in your mind against me. The gods know that I have done all this for the preservation of your life. You would see the reasonableness of my conduct throughout if I had the liberty of stating my reasons." "And why are you not at liberty ?" asked the prince ; "who has shut up your mouth ?" "It is destiny that has shut up my mouth," answered the minister's son ; "if I were to tell it all, I should be transformed into a marble statue." "You would be transformed into a marble statue !" exclaimed the prince ; "you must take me to be a simpleton to believe this nonsense." "Do you wish me then, friend," said the minister's son, "to tell you all ? You must then make up your mind to see your friend turned into stone." "Come, out with it," said the prince, "or else you are a dead man." The minister's son, in order to clear himself of the foul accusation brought against him, deemed it his duty to reveal the secret at the risk of his life.

He again and again warned the prince not to press him. But the prince remained inexorable. The minister's son then went on to say that, while bivouacking under a lofty tree one night, he had overheard a conversation between Bihangama and Bihangami, in which the former predicted all the dangers that were to threaten the life of the prince. When the minister's son had related the prediction concerning the mounting upon the elephant, his lower parts were turned into stone. He then, turning to the prince, said, "See, friend, my lower parts have already turned into stone." "Go on, go on," said the prince, "with your story." The minister's son then related the prophecy regarding the destruction of the lion-gate, when half of his body was converted into stone. He then related the prediction regarding the eating of the head of the fish, when his body up to his neck was petrified. "Now, friend," said the minister's son, "the whole of my body, excepting my neck and head, is petrified; if I tell the rest, I shall assuredly become a man of stone. Do you wish me still to go on?" "Go on," answered the prince, "go on." "Very well, I will go on to the end," said the minister's son; "but in case you repent after I have become turned into stone, and wish me to be restored to life, I will tell you of the manner in which it may be effected. The princess after a few months will be delivered of a child; if immediately after the birth of the infant you kill it and besmear my marble body with its blood, I shall be restored to life." He then related the prediction regarding the serpent in the bedroom; and when the last word was on his lips the rest of his body was turned into stone, and he dropped on the floor a marble image. The princess jumped out of bed, opened the vessel for betel-leaves and spices, and saw there pieces of a serpent. Both the prince and the princess now became convinced of the good faith and benevolence of their departed friend. They went to the marble figure, but it was lifeless. They set up a loud lamentation; but it was to no purpose, for the marble moved not. They then resolved to keep the marble figure concealed in a safe place, and to besmear it with the blood of their first-born child when it should be ushered into existence.

In process of time the hour of the princess's travail came on, and she was delivered of a beautiful boy, the perfect image of his mother. Both father and mother were struck with the beauty of their child, and would fain have spared its life; but recollecting the vows they had made on behalf of their best friend, now lying in a corner of the room a lifeless stone, and the inestimable services he had rendered to both of them, they cut the child into two, and besmeared the marble figure of the minister's son with its blood. The marble became animated in a moment. The minister's son stood before the prince and princess, who became exceedingly glad to see their old friend again in life. But the minister's son, who saw the lovely new-born babe lying in a pool of blood, was overwhelmed with grief. He took up the dead infant, carefully wrapped it up in a towel, and resolved to get it restored to life.

The minister's son, intent on the reanimation of his friend's child, consulted all the physicians of the country; but they said that they would undertake to cure any person of any disease so long as life was in him, but when life was extinct, the case was beyond their jurisdiction. The minister's son at last bethought himself of his own wife, who was living in a distant town, and who was a devoted worshipper of the goddess Kali, who, through his wife's intercession, might be prevailed upon to give life to the dead child. He, accordingly, set out on a journey to the town in which his wife was living in her father's house. Adjoining that house there was a garden where upon a tree he hung the dead child wrapped up in a towel. His wife was overjoyed to see her husband after so long a time; but to her surprise she found that he was very melancholy, that he spoke very little, and that he was brooding over something in his mind. She asked the reason of his melancholy, but he kept quiet. One night while they were lying together in bed, the wife got up and opening the door went out. The husband, who had little sleep any night in consequence of the weight of anxiety regarding the reanimation of his friend's child, perceiving his wife go out at that dead hour of night, determined to follow her without being noticed. She went to a temple of the goddess Kali, which was at no great distance from her house. She worshipped the goddess with flowers and sandal-wood perfume, and said, "O mother Kali! have mercy upon me, and deliver me out of all my troubles." The goddess replied, "Why, what further grievance have you? You long prayed for the return of your husband, and he has returned; what aileth thee now?" The woman answered, "True, O Mother, my husband has come to me, but he is very moody and melancholy, hardly speaks to me, takes no delight in me, only sits moping in a corner." To which the goddess rejoined, "Ask your husband what the reason of his melancholy is, and let me know it." The minister's son overheard the conversation between the goddess and his wife, but he did not make his appearance; he quietly slunk away before his wife and went to bed. The following day the wife asked her husband of the cause of his melancholy; and he related all the particulars regarding the killing of the infant child of the prince. Next night at the same dead hour the wife proceeded to Kali's temple and mentioned to the goddess the reason of her husband's melancholy; on which the goddess said, "Bring the child here and I will restore it to life." On the succeeding night the child was produced before the goddess Kali, and she called it back to life. Entranced with joy, the minister's son took up the reanimated child, went as fast as his legs could carry him to the prince and princess, and presented to them their child alive and well. They all rejoiced with exceeding great joy, and lived together happily till the day of their death.

Thus my story endeth,
The Natiya-thorn withereth, etc.

III

THE INDIGENT BRAHMAN

THERE was a Brahman who had a wife and four children. He was very poor. With no resources in the world, he lived chiefly on the benefactions of the rich. His gains were considerable when marriages were celebrated or funeral ceremonies were performed; but as his parishioners did not marry every day, neither did they die every day, he found it difficult to make the two ends meet. His wife often rebuked him for his inability to give her adequate support, and his children often went about naked and hungry. But though poor he was a good man. He was diligent in his devotions; and there was not a single day in his life in which he did not say his prayers at stated hours. His tutelary deity was the goddess Durga, the consort of Siva, the creative Energy of the Universe. On no day did he either drink water or taste food till he had written in red ink the name of Durga at least one hundred and eight times; while throughout the day he incessantly uttered the ejaculation, "O Durga! O Durga! have mercy upon me." Whenever he felt anxious on account of his poverty and his inability to support his wife and children, he groaned out—"Durga! Durga! Durga!"

One day, being very sad, he went to a forest many miles distant from the village in which he lived, and indulging his grief wept bitter tears. He prayed in the following manner:—"O Durga! O Mother Bhagavati! wilt thou not make an end of my misery? Were I alone in the world, I should not have been sad on account of poverty; but thou hast given me a wife and children. Give me, O Mother, the means to support them." It so happened that on that day and on that very spot the god Siva and his wife Durga were taking their morning walk. The goddess Durga, on seeing the Brahman at a distance, said to her divine husband—"O Lord of Kailas! do you see that Brahman? He is always taking my name on his lips and offering the prayer that I should deliver him out of his troubles. Can we not, my lord, do something for the poor Brahman, oppressed as he is with the cares of a growing family? We should give him enough to make him comfortable. As the poor man and his family have never enough to eat, I propose that you give him a *handi*[1] which should yield him an inexhaustible supply of *mudki*."[2] The lord of Kailas readily agreed to the proposal of his divine consort, and by his decree created on the spot a *handi* possessing the required quality. Durga then, calling the Brahman to her,

[1] *Handi* is an earthen pot, generally used in cooking food.
[2] *Mudki*, fried paddy boiled dry in treacle or sugar.

said,—"O Brahman! I have often thought of your pitiable case. Your repeated prayers have at last moved my compassion. Here is a *handi* for you. When you turn it upside down and shake it, it will pour down a never-ceasing shower of the finest *mudki*, which will not end till you restore the *handi* to its proper position. Yourself, your wife, and your children can eat as much *mudki* as you like, and you can also sell as much as you like." The Brahman, delighted beyond measure at obtaining so inestimable a treasure, made obeisance to the goddess, and, taking the *handi* in his hand, proceeded towards his house as fast as his legs could carry him. But he had not gone many yards when he thought of testing the efficacy of the wonderful vessel. Accordingly he turned the *handi* upside down and shook it, when, lo, and behold! a quantity of the finest *mudki* he had ever seen fell to the ground. He tied the sweetmeat in his sheet and walked on. It was now noon, and the Brahman was hungry; but he could not eat without his ablutions and his prayers. As he saw in the way an inn, and not far from it a tank, he purposed to halt there that he might bathe, say his prayers, and then eat the much-desired *mudki*. The Brahman sat at the innkeeper's shop, put the *handi* near him, smoked tobacco, besmeared his body with mustard oil, and before proceeding to bathe in the adjacent tank gave the *handi* in charge to the innkeeper, begging him again and again to take especial care of it.

When the Brahman went to his bath and his

devotions, the innkeeper thought it strange that he should be so careful as to the safety of his earthen vessel. There must be something valuable in the *handi*, he thought, otherwise why should the Brahman take so much thought about it? His curiosity being excited he opened the *handi*, and to his surprise found that it contained nothing. What can be the meaning of this? thought the innkeeper within himself. Why should the Brahman care so much for an empty *handi*? He took up the vessel, and began to examine it carefully; and when, in the course of examination, he turned the *handi* upside down, a quantity of the finest *mudki* fell from it, and went on falling without intermission. The innkeeper called his wife and children to witness this unexpected stroke of good fortune. The showers of the sugared fried paddy were so copious that they filled all the vessels and jars of the innkeeper. He resolved to appropriate to himself this precious *handi*, and accordingly put in its place another *handi* of the same size and make. The ablutions and devotions of the Brahman being now over, he came to the shop in wet clothes reciting holy texts of the Vedas. Putting on dry clothes, he wrote on a sheet of paper the name of Durga one hundred and eight times in red ink; after which he broke his fast on the *mudki* his *handi* had already given him. Thus refreshed, and being about to resume his journey homewards, he called for his *handi*, which the innkeeper delivered to him, adding—"There, sir, is your *handi*; it is just where you put it; no one has touched it." The Brahman, without suspecting anything, took up the *handi* and proceeded on his journey ; and as he walked on, he congratulated himself on his singular good fortune. "How agreeably," he thought within himself, "will my poor wife be surprised ! How greedily the children will devour the *mudki* of heaven's own manufacture ! I shall soon become rich, and lift up my head with the best of them all." The pains of travelling were considerably alleviated by these joyful anticipations. He reached his house, and calling his wife and children, said—"Look now at what I have brought. This *handi* that you see is an unfailing source of wealth and contentment. You will see what a stream of the finest *mudki* will flow from it when I turn it upside down." The Brahman's good wife, hearing of *mudki* falling from the *handi* unceasingly, thought that her husband must have gone mad ; and she was confirmed in her opinion when she found that nothing fell from the vessel though it was turned upside down again and again. Overwhelmed with grief, the Brahman concluded that the innkeeper must have played a trick with him ; he must have stolen the *handi* Durga had given him, and put a common one in its stead. He went back the next day to the innkeeper, and charged him with having changed his *handi*. The innkeeper put on a fit of anger, expressed surprise at the Brahman's impudence in charging him with theft, and drove him away from his shop.

The Brahman then bethought himself of an

interview with the goddess Durga who had given him the *handi*, and accordingly went to the forest where he had met her. Siva and Durga again favoured the Brahman with an interview. Durga said—"So, you have lost the *handi* I gave you. Here is another, take it and make good use of it." The Brahman, elated with joy, made obeisance to the divine couple, took up the vessel, and went on his way. He had not gone far when he turned it upside down, and shook it in order to see whether any *mudki* would fall from it. Horror of horrors! instead of sweetmeats about a score of demons, of gigantic size and grim visage, jumped out of the *handi*, and began to belabour the astonished Brahman with blows, fisticuffs and kicks. He had the presence of mind to turn up the *handi* and to cover it, when the demons forthwith disappeared. He concluded that this new *handi* had been given him only for the punishment of the innkeeper. He accordingly went to the innkeeper, gave him the new *handi* in charge, begged of him carefully to keep it till he returned from his ablutions and prayers. The innkeeper, delighted with this second godsend, called his wife and children, and said—"This is another *handi* brought here by the same Brahman who brought the *handi* of *mudki*. This time, I hope, it is not *mudki* but *sandesa*.[1] Come, be ready with baskets and vessels, and I'll turn the *handi* upside down and shake it." This was no sooner done than scores of fierce demons started up, who caught hold of the inn-

[1] A sort of sweetmeat made of curds and sugar.

" Instead of sweetmeats about a score of demons."

WARWICK GOBLE

keeper and his family and belaboured them mercilessly. They also began upsetting the shop, and would have completely destroyed it, if the victims had not besought the Brahman, who had by this time returned from his ablutions, to show mercy to them and send away the terrible demons. The Brahman acceded to the innkeeper's request, he dismissed the demons by shutting up the vessel; he got the former *handi*, and with the two *handis* went to his native village.

On reaching home the Brahman shut the door of his house, turned the *mudki-handi* upside down, and shook it; the result was an unceasing stream of the finest *mudki* that any confectioner in the country could produce. The man, his wife, and their children devoured the sweetmeat to their hearts' content; all the available earthen pots and pans of the house were filled with it; and the Brahman resolved the next day to turn confectioner, to open a shop in his house, and sell *mudki*. On the very day the shop was opened, the whole village came to the Brahman's house to buy the wonderful *mudki*. They had never seen such *mudki* in their life, it was so sweet, so white, so large, so luscious; no confectioner in the village or any town in the country had ever manufactured anything like it. The reputation of the Brahman's *mudki* extended, in a few days, beyond the bounds of the village, and people came from remote parts to purchase it. Cartloads of the sweetmeat were sold every day, and the Brahman in a short time became very rich. He built a large brick house, and lived like a nobleman of the land. Once, however, his property was about to go to wreck and ruin. His children one day by mistake shook the wrong *handi*, when a large number of demons dropped down and caught hold of the Brahman's wife and children and were striking them mercilessly, when happily the Brahman came into the house and turned up the *handi*. In order to prevent a similar catastrophe in future, the Brahman shut up the demon-*handi* in a private room to which his children had no access.

Pure and uninterrupted prosperity, however, is not the lot of mortals; and though the demon-*handi* was put aside, what security was there that an accident might not befall the *mudki-handi*? One day, during the absence of the Brahman and his wife from the house, the children decided upon shaking the *handi*; but as each of them wished to enjoy the pleasure of shaking it there was a general struggle to get it, and in the *mêlée* the *handi* fell to the ground and broke. It is needless to say that the Brahman, when on reaching home he heard of the disaster, became inexpressibly sad. The children were of course well cudgelled, but no flogging of children could replace the magical *handi*. After some days he again went to the forest, and offered many a prayer for Durga's favour. At last Siva and Durga again appeared to him, and heard how the *handi* had been broken. Durga gave him another *handi*, accompanied with the following caution—"Brahman, take care of this *handi*; if you again break it or lose it, I'll not give you another." The Brahman made obeisance, and went away to his house at one stretch without halting anywhere. On reaching home he shut the door of his house, called his wife to him, turned the *handi* upside down, and began to shake it. They were only expecting *mudki* to drop from it, but instead of *mudki* a perennial stream of beautiful *sandesa* issued from it. And such *sandesa* ! No confectioner of Burra Bazar ever made its like. It was more the food of gods than of men. The Brahman forthwith set up a shop for selling *sandesa*, the fame of which soon drew crowds of customers from all parts of the country. At all festivals, at all marriage feasts, at all funeral celebrations, at all *Pujas*, no one bought any other *sandesa* than the Brahman's. Every day, and every hour, many jars of gigantic size, filled with the delicious sweetmeat, were sent to all parts of the country.

The wealth of the Brahman excited the envy of the Zemindar of the village, who, having heard that the *sandesa* was not manufactured but dropped from a *handi*, devised a plan for getting possession of the miraculous vessel. At the celebration of his son's marriage he held a great feast, to which were invited hundreds of people. As many mountain-loads of *sandesa* would be required for the purpose, the Zemindar proposed that the Brahman should bring the magical *handi* to the house in which the feast was held. The Brahman at first refused to take it there ; but as the Zemindar insisted on its being carried to his own house, he reluctantly consented to take it there. After many Himalayas of *sandesa* had been shaken out, the *handi* was taken possession of by the Zemindar, and the Brahman was insulted and driven out of the house. The Brahman, without giving vent to anger in the least, quietly went to his house, and taking the demon-*handi* in his hand, came back to the door of the Zemindar's house. He turned the *handi* upside down and shook it, on which a hundred demons started up as from the vasty deep and enacted a scene which it is impossible to describe. The hundreds of guests that had been bidden to the feast were caught hold of by the unearthly visitants and beaten ; the women were dragged by their hair from the Zenana and dashed about amongst the men ; while the big and burly Zemindar was driven about from room to room like a bale of cotton. If the demons had been allowed to do their will only for a few minutes longer, all the men would have been killed, and the very house razed to the ground. The Zemindar fell prostrate at the feet of the Brahman and begged for mercy. Mercy was shown him, and the demons were removed. After that the Brahman was no more disturbed by the Zemindar or by any one else ; and he lived many years in great happiness and enjoyment.

Thus my story endeth,
The Natiya-thorn withereth, etc.

IV

THE STORY OF THE RAKSHASAS

THERE was a poor half-witted Brahman who had a wife but no children. It was only with difficulty he could supply the wants of himself and his wife. And the worst of it was that he was rather lazily inclined. He was averse to taking long journeys, otherwise he might always have had enough, in the shape of presents from rich men, to enable him and his wife to live comfortably. There was at that time a king in a neighbouring country who was celebrating the funeral obsequies of his mother with great pomp. Brahmans and beggars were going from different parts with the expectation of receiving rich presents. Our Brahman was requested by his wife to seize this opportunity and get a little money ; but his constitutional indolence stood in the way. The woman, however, gave her husband no rest till she extorted from him the promise that he would go. The good woman, accordingly, cut down a plantain tree and burnt it to ashes, with which ashes she cleaned the clothes of her husband, and made them as white as any fuller could make them. She did this because her husband was going to the palace of a great king, who could not be approached by men clothed in dirty rags; besides, as a Brahman, he was bound to appear neat and clean. The Brahman at last one morning left his house for the palace of the great king. As he was somewhat imbecile, he did not inquire of any one which road he should take; but he went on and on, and proceeded whithersoever his two eyes directed him. He was of course not on the right road, indeed he had reached a region where he did not meet with a single human being for many miles, and where he saw sights which he had never seen in his life. He saw hillocks of *cowris* (shells used as money) on the roadside: he had not proceeded far from them when he saw hillocks of pice, then successively hillocks of four-anna pieces, hillocks of eight-anna pieces, and hillocks of rupees. To the infinite surprise of the poor Brahman, these hillocks of shining silver coins were succeeded by a large hill of burnished gold-mohurs, which were all as bright as if they had been just issued from the mint. Close to this hill of gold-mohurs was a large house which seemed to be the palace of a powerful and rich king, at the door of which stood a lady of exquisite beauty. The lady, seeing the Brahman, said, 'Come, my beloved husband; you married me when I was young, and you never came once after our marriage, though I have been daily expecting you. Blessed be this day which has made me see the face of my husband. Come, my sweet, come in, wash your feet and rest after the fatigues of your journey; eat and drink,

"At the door of which stood a lady of exquisite beauty."

and after that we shall make ourselves merry." The Brahman was astonished beyond measure. He had no recollection of having been married in early youth to any other woman than the woman who was now keeping house with him. But being a Kulin Brahman, he thought it was quite possible that his father had got him married when he was a little child, though the fact had made no impression on his mind. But whether he remembered it or not, the fact was certain, for the woman declared that she was his wedded wife,—and such a wife! as beautiful as the goddesses of Indra's heaven, and no doubt as wealthy as she was beautiful. While these thoughts were passing through the Brahman's mind, the lady said again, "Are you doubting in your mind whether I am your wife? Is it possible that all recollection of that happy event has been effaced from your mind—all the pomp and circumstance of our nuptials? Come in, beloved; this is your own house, for whatever is mine is thine." The Brahman succumbed to the loving entreaties of the fair lady, and went into the house. The house was not an ordinary one—it was a magnificent palace, all the apartments being large and lofty and richly furnished. But one thing surprised the Brahman very much, and that was that there was no other person in the house besides the lady herself. He could not account for so singular a phenomenon; neither could he explain how it was that he did not meet with any human being in his morning and evening walks. The fact was that the lady was not a human being. She was a

Rakshasi.[1] She had eaten up the king, the queen, and all the members of the royal family, and gradually all his subjects. This was the reason why human beings were not seen in those parts.

The Rakshasi and the Brahman lived together for about a week, when the former said to the latter, "I am very anxious to see my sister, your other wife. You must go and fetch her, and we shall all live together happily in this large and beautiful house. You must go early to-morrow, and I will give you clothes and jewels for her." Next morning the Brahman, furnished with fine clothes and costly ornaments, set out for his home. The poor woman was in great distress; all the Brahmans and Pandits that had been to the funeral ceremony of the king's mother had returned home loaded with largesses; but her husband had not returned,—and no one could give any news of him, for no one had seen him there. The woman therefore concluded that he must have been murdered on the road by highwaymen. She was in this terrible suspense, when one day she heard a rumour in the village that her husband was seen coming home with fine clothes and costly jewels for his wife. And sure enough the Brahman soon appeared with his valuable load. On seeing his wife the Brahman thus accosted her:—"Come with me, my dearest wife; I have found my first wife. She lives in a stately palace, near which are

[1] *Rakshasas* and *Rakshasis* (male and female) are in Hindu mythology huge giants and giantesses, or rather demons. The word means literally *raw-eaters*; they were probably the chiefs of the aborigines whom the Aryans overthrew on their first settlement in the country.

hillocks of rupees and a large hill of gold-mohurs. Why should you pine away in wretchedness and misery in this horrible place? Come with me to the house of my first wife, and we shall all live together happily." When the woman heard her husband speak of his first wife, of hillocks of rupees and of a hill of gold-mohurs, she thought in her mind that her half-witted good man had become quite mad; but when she saw the exquisitely beautiful silks and satins and the ornaments set with diamonds and precious stones, which only queens and princesses were in the habit of putting on, she concluded in her mind that her poor husband had fallen into the meshes of a Rakshasi. The Brahman, however, insisted on his wife's going with him, and declared that if she did not come she was at liberty to pine away in poverty, but that for himself he meant to return forthwith to his first and rich wife. The good woman, after a great deal of altercation with her husband, resolved to go with him and judge for herself how matters stood. They set out accordingly the next morning, and went by the same road on which the Brahman had travelled. The woman was not a little surprised to see hillocks of *cowris*, of pice, of eight-anna pieces, of rupees, and last of all a lofty hill of gold-mohurs. She saw also an exceedingly beautiful lady coming out of the palace hard by, and hastening towards her. The lady fell on the neck of the Brahman woman, wept tears of joy, and said, "Welcome, beloved sister! this is the happiest day of my life! I have seen the face of my dearest sister!" The party then entered the palace.

What with the stately mansion in which he was lodged, with the most delectable provisions which seemed to rise as if by enchantment, what with the caresses and endearments of his two wives, the one human and the other demoniac, who vied with each other in making him happy and comfortable, the Brahman had a jolly time of it. He was steeped as it were in an ocean of enjoyment. Some fifteen or sixteen years were spent by the Brahman in this state of Elysian pleasure, during which period his two wives presented him with two sons. The Rakshasi's son, who was the elder, and who looked more like a god than a human being, was named Sahasra Dal, literally the Thousand-Branched; and the son of the Brahman woman, who was a year younger, was named Champa Dal, that is, branch of a *champaka* tree. The two boys loved each other dearly. They were both sent to a school which was several miles distant, to which they used every day to go riding on two little ponies of extraordinary fleetness.

The Brahman woman had all along suspected from a thousand little circumstances that her sister-in-law was not a human being but a Rakshasi; but her suspicion had not yet ripened into certainty, for the Rakshasi exercised great self-restraint on herself, and never did anything which human beings did not do. But the demoniac nature, like murder, will out. The Brahman having nothing to do, in order to pass his time had recourse to hunting. The first day he returned from the hunt, he had bagged an antelope. The antelope was laid in the courtyard of the palace. At the sight of the antelope the mouth of the raw-eating Rakshasi began to water. Before the animal was dressed for the kitchen, she took it away into a room, and began devouring it. The Brahman woman, who was watching the whole scene from a secret place, saw her Rakshasi sister tear off a leg of the antelope, and opening her tremendous jaws, which seemed to her imagination to extend from earth to heaven, swallow it up. In this manner the body and other limbs of the antelope were devoured, till only a little bit of the meat was kept for the kitchen. The second day another antelope was bagged, and the third day another; and the Rakshasi, unable to restrain her appetite for raw flesh, devoured these two as she had devoured the first. On the third day the Brahman woman expressed to the Rakshasi her surprise at the disappearance of nearly the whole of the antelope with the exception of a little bit. The Rakshasi looked fierce and said, "Do I eat raw flesh?" To which the Brahman woman replied, "Perhaps you do, for aught I know to the contrary." The Rakshasi, knowing herself to be discovered, looked fiercer than before, and vowed revenge. The Brahman woman concluded in her mind that the doom of herself, of her husband, and of her son was sealed. She spent a miserable night, believing that next day she would be killed and eaten up, and that her husband and son would share the same fate. Early next morning, before her son Champa Dal went to school, she gave him in a small golden vessel a little quantity of her own breast milk, and told him to be constantly watching its colour. "Should you," she said, "see the milk get a little red, then conclude that your father has been killed; and should you see it grow still redder, then conclude that I am killed: when you see this, gallop away for your life as fast as your horse can carry you, for if you do not, you also will be devoured."

The Rakshasi on getting up from bed—and she had prevented the Brahman overnight from having any communication with his wife—proposed that she and the Brahman should go to bathe in the river, which was at some distance. She would take no denial; the Brahman had therefore to follow her as meekly as a lamb. The Brahman woman at once saw from the proposal that ruin was impending; but it was beyond her power to avert the catastrophe. The Rakshasi, on the riverside, assuming her own proper gigantic dimensions, took hold of the ill-fated Brahman, tore him limb by limb, and devoured him up. She then ran to her house, and seized the Brahman woman, and put her into her capacious stomach, clothes, hair and all. Young Champa Dal, who, agreeably to his mother's instructions, was diligently watching the milk in the small golden vessel, was horror-struck to find the milk redden a little. He set up a cry and said that his father was killed; a few minutes after, finding the milk become completely red, he cried yet louder, and rushing to his pony, mounted it. His half-brother, Sahasra Dal, surprised at Champa Dal's conduct, said, "Where are you going, Champa? Why are you crying? Let me accompany you." "Oh! do not come to me. Your mother has devoured my father and mother; don't you come and devour me." "I will not devour you; I'll save you." Scarcely had he uttered these words and galloped away after Champa Dal, when he saw his mother in her own Rakshasi form appearing at a distance, and demanding that Champa Dal should come to her. He said, "I will come to you, not Champa." So saying, he went to his mother, and with his sword, which he always wore as a young prince, cut off her head.

Champa Dal had, in the meantime, galloped off a good distance, as he was running for his life; but Sahasra Dal, by pricking his horse repeatedly, soon overtook him, and told him that his mother was no more. This was small consolation to Champa Dal, as the Rakshasi, before being killed, had devoured both his father and mother; still he could not but feel that Sahasra Dal's friendship was sincere. They both rode fast, and as their horses were of the breed of *pakshirajes* (literally, kings of birds), they travelled over hundreds of miles. An hour or two before sundown they descried a village, to which they made up, and became guests in the house of one of its most respectable inhabitants. The two friends found the members of that respectable family in deep gloom. Evidently there was something agitating them very much.

Some of them held private consultations, and others were weeping. The eldest lady of the house, the mother of its head, said aloud, "Let me go, as I am the eldest. I have lived long enough; at the utmost my life would be cut short only by a year or two." The youngest member of the house, who was a little girl, said, "Let me go, as I am young and useless to the family; if I die I shall not be missed." The head of the house, the son of the old lady, said, "I am the head and representative of the family; it is but reasonable that I should give up my life." His younger brother said, "You are the main prop and pillar of the family; if you go the whole family is ruined. It is not reasonable that you should go; let me go, as I shall not be much missed." The two strangers listened to all this conversation with no little curiosity. They wondered what it all meant. Sahasra Dal at last, at the risk of being thought meddlesome, ventured to ask the head of the house the subject of their consultations, and the reason of the deep misery but too visible in their countenances and words. The head of the house gave the following answer: "Know then, worthy guests, that this part of the country is infested by a terrible Rakshasi, who has depopulated all the regions round. This town, too, would have been depopulated, but that our king became a suppliant before the Rakshasi, and begged her to show mercy to us his subjects. The Rakshasi replied, 'I will consent to show mercy to you and to your subjects only on this condition, that you every night put a human being, either male or female, in a certain temple for me to feast upon. If I get a human being every night I will rest satisfied, and not commit any further depredations on your subjects.' Our king had no other alternative than to agree to this condition, for what human beings can ever hope to contend against a Rakshasi? From that day the king made it a rule that every family in the town should in its turn send one of its members to the temple as a victim to appease the wrath and to satisfy the hunger of the terrible Rakshasi. All the families in this neighbourhood have had their turn, and this night it is the turn for one of us to devote himself to destruction. We are therefore discussing who should go. You must now perceive the cause of our distress." The two friends consulted together for a few minutes, and at the conclusion of their consultations, Sahasra Dal, who was the spokesman of the party, said, "Most worthy host, do not any longer be sad: as you have been very kind to us, we have resolved to requite your hospitality by ourselves going to the temple and becoming the food of the Rakshasi. We go as your representatives." The whole family protested against the proposal. They declared that guests were like gods, and that it was the duty of the host to endure all sorts of privation for the comfort of the guest, and not the duty of the guest to suffer for the host. But the two strangers insisted on standing proxy to the family, who, after a great deal of yea and nay, at last consented to the arrangement.

Immediately after candle-light, Sahasra Dal and Champa Dal, with their two horses, installed themselves in the temple, and shut the door. Sahasra told his brother to go to sleep, as he himself was determined to sit up the whole night and watch against the coming of the terrible Rakshasi. Champa was soon in a fine sleep, while Sahasra lay awake. Nothing happened during the early hours of the night, but no sooner had the gong of the king's palace announced the dead hour of midnight than Sahasra heard the sound as of a rushing tempest, and immediately concluded, from his knowledge of Rǎkshasas, that the Rakshasi was nigh. A thundering knock was heard at the door, accompanied with the following words :—

"*How, mow, khow!*
A human being I smell;
Who watches inside?"

To this question Sahasra Dal made the following reply :—

"*Sahasra Dal watcheth,*
Champa Dal watcheth,
Two winged horses watch."

On hearing this answer the Rakshasi turned away with a groan, knowing that Sahasra Dal had Rakshasa blood in his veins. An hour after, the Rakshasi returned, thundered at the door, and called out—

"*How, mow, khow !*
A human being I smell ;
Who watcheth inside ?"

Sahasra Dal again replied—

"*Sahasra Dal watcheth,*
Champa Dal watcheth,
Two winged horses watch."

The Rakshasi again groaned and went away. At two o'clock and at three o'clock the Rakshasi again and again made her appearance, and made the usual inquiry, and obtaining the same answer, went away with a groan. After three o'clock, however, Sahasra Dal felt very sleepy : he could not any longer keep awake. He therefore roused Champa, told him to watch, and strictly enjoined upon him, in reply to the query of the Rakshasi, to mention Sahasra's name first. With these instructions he went to sleep. At four o'clock the Rakshasi again made her appearance, thundered at the door, and said—

"*How, mow, khow !*
A human being I smell ;
Who watches inside ?"

As Champa Dal was in a terrible fright, he forgot the instructions of his brother for the moment, and answered—

"Champa Dal watcheth,
Sahasra Dal watcheth,
Two winged horses watch."

On hearing this reply the Rakshasi uttered a shout of exultation, laughed such a laugh as only demons can, and with a dreadful noise broke open the door. The noise roused Sahasra, who in a moment sprung to his feet, and with his sword, which was as supple as a palm-leaf, cut off the head of the Rakshasi. The huge mountain of a body fell to the ground, making a great noise, and lay covering many an acre. Sahasra Dal kept the severed head of the Rakshasi near him, and went to sleep. Early in the morning some wood-cutters, who were passing near the temple, saw the huge body on the ground. They could not from a distance make out what it was, but on coming near they knew that it was the carcase of the terrible Rakshasi, who had by her voracity nearly depopulated the country. Remembering the promise made by the king that the killer of the Rakshasi should be rewarded by the hand of his daughter and with a share of the kingdom, each of the wood-cutters, seeing no claimant at hand, thought of obtaining the reward. Accordingly each of them cut off a part of a limb of the huge carcase, went to the king, and represented himself to be the destroyer of the great raw-eater, and claimed the reward. The king, in order to find out the real hero and deliverer, inquired of his minister the name of the family whose turn it was on the preceding night to offer a victim to the Rakshasi. The head of that family, on being brought before the king, related how two youthful travellers, who were guests in his house, volunteered to go into the temple in the room of a member of his family. The door of the temple was broken open ; Sahasra Dal and Champa Dal and their horses were found all safe ; and the head of the Rakshasi, which was with them, proved beyond the shadow of a doubt that they had killed the monster. The king kept his word. He gave his daughter in marriage to Sahasra Dal and the sovereignty of half his dominions. Champa Dal remained with his friend in the king's palace, and rejoiced in his prosperity.

Sahasra Dal and Champa Dal lived together happily for some time, when a misunderstanding arose between them in this wise. There was in the service of the queen-mother a certain maidservant who was the most useful domestic in the palace. There was nothing which she could not put her hands to and perform. She had uncommon strength for a woman ; neither was her intelligence of a mean order. She was a woman of immense activity and energy ; and if she were absent one day from the palace, the affairs of the zenana would be in perfect disorder. Hence her services were highly valued by the queen-mother and all the ladies of the palace. But this woman was not a woman ; she was a Rakshasi, who had put on the appearance of a woman to serve some purposes of her own, and then taken service in the royal household. At night, when every one in the palace was asleep, she used to assume her own real form, and go about in quest of food, for the quantity of food that is sufficient for either man or woman was not sufficient for a Rakshasi. Now Champa Dal, having no wife, was in the habit of sleeping outside the zenana, and not far from the outer gate of the palace. He had noticed her going about on the premises and devouring sundry goats and sheep, horses and elephants. The maid-servant, finding that Champa Dal was in the way of her supper, determined to get rid of him. She accordingly went one day to the queen-mother, and said, "Queen-mother! I am unable any longer to work in the palace." "Why? what is the matter, Dasi?[1] How can I get on without you? Tell me your reasons. What ails you?" "Why," said the woman, "nowadays it is impossible for a poor woman like me to preserve my honour in the palace. There is that Champa Dal, the friend of your son-in-law; he always cracks indecent jokes with me. It is better for me to beg for my rice than to lose my honour. If Champa Dal remains in the palace I must go away." As the maid-servant was an absolute necessity in the palace, the queen-mother resolved to sacrifice Champa Dal to her. She therefore told Sahasra Dal that Champa Dal was a bad man, that his character was loose, and that therefore he must leave the palace. Sahasra Dal earnestly pleaded on behalf of his friend, but in vain; the queen-mother had made

[1] *Dasi* is a general name for all maid-servants.

WARWICK GOBLE

"In a trice she woke up, sat up in her bed, and eyeing the stranger, inquired who he was."

up her mind to drive him out of the palace. Sahasra Dal had not the courage to speak personally to his friend on the subject; he therefore wrote a letter to him, in which he simply said that for certain reasons Champa must leave the palace immediately. The letter was put in his room after he had gone to bathe. On reading the letter Champa Dal, exceedingly grieved, mounted his fleet horse and left the palace.

As Champa's horse was uncommonly fleet, in a few hours he traversed thousands of miles, and at last found himself at the gateway of what seemed a magnificent palace. Dismounting from his horse, he entered the house, where he did not meet with a single creature. He went from apartment to apartment, but though they were all richly furnished he did not see a single human being. At last, in one of the side rooms, he found a young lady of heavenly beauty lying down on a splendid bedstead. She was asleep. Champa Dal looked upon the sleeping beauty with rapture—he had not seen any woman so beautiful. Upon the bed, near the head of the young lady, were two sticks, one of silver and the other of gold. Champa took the silver stick into his hand, and touched with it the body of the lady; but no change was perceptible. He then took up the gold stick and laid it upon the lady, when in a trice she woke up, sat in her bed, and eyeing the stranger, inquired who he was. Champa Dal briefly told his story. The young lady, or rather princess—for she was nothing less—said, "Unhappy man! why have you come here? This is the country of Rakshasas, and in this house and round about there live no less than seven hundred Rakshasas. They all go away to the other side of the ocean every morning in search of provisions; and they all return every evening before dusk. My father was formerly king in these regions, and had millions of subjects, who lived in flourishing towns and cities. But some years ago the invasion of the Rakshasas took place, and they devoured all his subjects, and himself and my mother, and my brothers and sisters. They devoured also all the cattle of the country. There is no living human being in these regions excepting myself; and I too should long ago have been devoured had not an old Rakshasi, conceiving strange affection for me, prevented the other Rakshasas from eating me up. You see those sticks of silver and gold; the old Rakshasi, when she goes away in the morning, kills me with the silver stick, and on her return in the evening re-animates me with the gold stick. I do not know how to advise you; if the Rakshasas see you, you are a dead man." Then they both talked to each other in a very affectionate manner, and laid their heads together to devise if possible some means of escape from the hands of the Rakshasas. The hour of the return of the seven hundred raw-eaters was fast approaching; and Keshavati—for that was the name of the princess, so called from the abundance of her hair—told Champa to hide himself in the heaps of the sacred trefoil which were lying in the temple of Siva in the central part of the palace. Before Champa went to his place of concealment, he touched Keshavati with the silver stick, on which she instantly died.

Shortly after sunset Champa Dal heard from beneath the heaps of the sacred trefoil the sound as of a mighty rushing wind. Presently he heard terrible noises in the palace. The Rakshasas had come home from cruising, after having filled their stomachs, each one, with sundry goats, sheep, cows, horses, buffaloes, and elephants. The old Rakshasi, of whom we have already spoken, came to Keshavati's room, roused her by touching her body with the gold stick, and said—

> " *Hye, mye, khye !*
> *A human being I smell.*"

On which Keshavati said, " I am the only human being here ; eat me if you like." To which the raw-eater replied, " Let me eat up your enemies ; why should I eat you ? " She laid herself down on the ground, as long and as high as the Vindhya Hills, and presently fell asleep. The other Rakshasas and Rakshasis also soon fell asleep, being all tired out on account of their gigantic labours in the day. Keshavati also composed herself to sleep ; while Champa, not daring to come out of the heaps of leaves, tried his best to court the god of repose. At daybreak all the raw-eaters, seven hundred in number, got up and went as usual to their hunting and predatory excursions, and along with them went the old Rakshasi, after touching

Keshavati with the silver stick. When Champa Dal saw that the coast was clear, he came out of the temple, walked into Keshavati's room, and touched her with the gold stick, on which she woke up. They sauntered about in the gardens, enjoying the cool breeze of the morning; they bathed in a lucid tank which was in the grounds; they ate and drank, and spent the day in sweet converse. They concocted a plan for their deliverance. They settled that Keshavati should ask the old Rakshasi on what the life of a Rakshasa depended, and when the secret should be made known they would adopt measures accordingly. As on the preceding evening, Champa, after touching his fair friend with the silver stick, took refuge in the temple beneath the heaps of the sacred trefoil. At dusk the Rakshasas as usual came home; and the old Rakshasi, rousing her pet, said—

"*Hye, mye, khye!*
A human being I smell."

Keshavati answered, "What other human being is here excepting myself? Eat me up, if you like." "Why should I eat you, my darling? Let me eat up all your enemies." Then she laid down on the ground her huge body, which looked like a part of the Himalaya mountains. Keshavati, with a phial of heated mustard oil, went towards the feet of the Rakshasi, and said, "Mother, your feet are sore with walking; let me rub them with oil." So saying, she began to rub with oil the Rakshasi's feet; and while she was in the act of doing so, a few tear-drops from her eyes fell on the monster's leg. The Rakshasi smacked the tear-drops with her lips, and finding the taste briny, said, "Why are you weeping, darling? What aileth thee?" To which the princess replied, "Mother, I am weeping because you are old, and when you die I shall certainly be devoured by one of the Rakshasas." "When I die! Know, foolish girl, that we Rakshasas never die. We are not naturally immortal, but our life depends on a secret which no human being can unravel. Let me tell you what it is that you may be comforted. You know yonder tank; there is in the middle of it a *Sphatika-sthambha*,[1] on the top of which in deep waters are two bees. If any human being can dive into the waters, and bring up to land the two bees from the pillar in one breath, and destroy them so that not a drop of their blood falls to the ground, then we Rakshasas shall certainly die; but if a single drop of blood falls to the ground, then from it will start up a thousand Rakshasas. But what human being will find out this secret, or, finding it, will be able to achieve the feat? You need not, therefore, darling, be sad; I am practically immortal." Keshavati treasured up the secret in her memory, and went to sleep.

Early next morning the Rakshasas as usual went away; Champa came out of his hiding-place, roused Keshavati, and fell a-talking. The princess told him the secret she had learnt from the Rakshasi. Champa immediately made prepara-

[1] *Sphatika* is crystal, and *sthambha* pillar.

tions for accomplishing the mighty deed. He brought to the side of the tank a knife and a quantity of ashes. He disrobed himself, put a drop or two of mustard oil into each of his ears to prevent water from entering in, and dived into the waters. In a moment he got to the top of the crystal pillar in the middle of the tank, caught hold of the two bees he found there, and came up in one breath. Taking the knife, he cut up the bees over the ashes, a drop or two of the blood fell, not on the ground, but on the ashes. When Champa caught hold of the bees, a terrible scream was heard at a distance. This was the wailing of the Rakshasas, who were all running home to prevent the bees from being killed; but before they could reach the palace, the bees had perished. The moment the bees were killed, all the Rakshasas died, and their carcases fell on the very spot on which they were standing. Champa and the princess afterwards found that the gateway of the palace was blocked up by the huge carcases of the Rakshasas—some of them having nearly succeeded in getting to the palace. In this manner was effected the destruction of the seven hundred Rakshasas.

After the destruction of the seven hundred raw-eating monsters, Champa Dal and Keshavati got married together by the exchange of garlands of flowers. The princess, who had never been out of the house, naturally expressed a desire to see the outer world. They used every day to take long walks both morning and evening, and as a large river was hard by Keshavati wished to bathe in it. The first day they went to bathe, one of Keshavati's hairs came off, and as it is the custom with women never to throw away a hair unaccompanied with something else, she tied the hair to a shell which was floating on the water; after which they returned home. In the meantime the shell with the hair tied to it floated down the stream, and in course of time reached that *ghat*[1] at which Sahasra Dal and his companions were in the habit of performing their ablutions. The shell passed by when Sahasra Dal and his friends were bathing; and he, seeing it at some distance, said to them, "Whoever succeeds in catching hold of yonder shell shall be rewarded with a hundred rupees." They all swam towards it, and Sahasra Dal, being the fleetest swimmer, got it. On examining it he found a hair tied to it. But such hair! He had never seen so long a hair. It was exactly seven cubits long. "The owner of this hair must be a remarkable woman, and I must see her"—such was the resolution of Sahasra Dal. He went home from the river in a pensive mood, and instead of proceeding to the zenana for breakfast, remained in the outer part of the palace. The queen-mother, on hearing that Sahasra Dal was looking melancholy and had not come to breakfast, went to him and asked the reason. He showed her the hair, and said he must see the woman whose head it had adorned. The queen-

[1] Bathing-place, either in a tank or on the bank of a river, generally furnished with flights of steps.

mother said, "Very well, you shall have that lady in the palace as soon as possible. I promise you to bring her here." The queen-mother told her favourite maid-servant, whom she knew to be full of resources—the same who was a Rakshasi in disguise—that she must, as soon as possible, bring to the palace that lady who was the owner of the hair seven cubits long. The maid-servant said she would be quite able to fetch her. By her directions a boat was built of *Hajol* wood, the oars of which were of *Mon Paban* wood. The boat was launched on the stream, and she went on board of it with some baskets of wicker-work of curious workmanship; she also took with her some sweetmeats into which some poison had been mixed. She snapped her fingers thrice, and uttered the following charm:—

> "*Boat of Hajol!*
> *Oars of Mon Paban!*
> *Take me to the Ghat,*
> *In which Keshavati bathes.*"

No sooner had the words been uttered than the boat flew like lightning over the waters. It went on and on, leaving behind many a town and city. At last it stopped at a bathing-place, which the Rakshasi maid-servant concluded was the bathing *ghat* of Keshavati. She landed with the sweetmeats in her hand. She went to the gate of the palace, and cried aloud, "O Keshavati! Keshavati! I am your aunt, your mother's sister. I am come to see you, my darling, after so many years.

Are you in, Keshavati ?" The princess, on hearing these words, came out of her room, and making no doubt that she was her aunt, embraced and kissed her. They both wept rivers of joy—at least the Rakshasi maid-servant did, and Keshavati followed suit through sympathy. Champa Dal also thought that she was the aunt of his newly married wife. They all ate and drank and took rest in the middle of the day. Champa Dal, as was his habit, went to sleep after breakfast. Towards afternoon, the supposed aunt said to Keshavati, "Let us both go to the river and wash ourselves." Keshavati replied, "How can we go now ? my husband is sleeping." "Never mind," said the aunt, "let him sleep on ; let me put these sweetmeats, that I have brought, near his bedside, that he may eat them when he gets up." They then went to the river-side close to the spot where the boat was. Keshavati, when she saw from some distance the baskets of wicker-work in the boat, said, "Aunt, what beautiful things are those ! I wish I could get some of them." "Come, my child, come and look at them ; and you can have as many as you like." Keshavati at first refused to go into the boat, but on being pressed by her aunt, she went. The moment they two were on board, the aunt snapped her fingers thrice and said :—

"*Boat of Hajol !*
Oars of Mon Paban !
Take me to the Ghat,
In which Sahasra Dal bathes."

As soon as these magical words were uttered the boat moved and flew like an arrow over the waters. Keshavati was frightened and began to cry, but the boat went on and on, leaving behind many towns and cities, and in a trice reached the *ghat* where Sahasra Dal was in the habit of bathing. Keshavati was taken to the palace; Sahasra Dal admired her beauty and the length of her hair; and the ladies of the palace tried their best to comfort her. But she set up a loud cry, and wanted to be taken back to her husband. At last when she saw that she was a captive, she told the ladies of the palace that she had taken a vow that she would not see the face of any strange man for six months. She was then lodged apart from the rest in a small house, the window of which overlooked the road; there she spent the livelong day and also the livelong night—for she had very little sleep—in sighing and weeping.

In the meantime when Champa Dal awoke from sleep, he was distracted with grief at not finding his wife. He now thought that the woman, who pretended to be his wife's aunt, was a cheat and an impostor, and that she must have carried away Keshavati. He did not eat the sweetmeats, suspecting they might be poisoned. He threw one of them to a crow which, the moment it ate it, dropped down dead. He was now the more confirmed in his unfavourable opinion of the pretended aunt. Maddened with grief, he rushed out of the house, and determined to go whithersoever his eyes might lead him.

Like a madman, always blubbering "O Keshavati! O Keshavati!" he travelled on foot day after day, not knowing whither he went. Six months were spent in this wearisome travelling when, at the end of that period, he reached the capital of Sahasra Dal. He was passing by the palace-gate when the sighs and wailings of a woman sitting at the window of a house, on the road-side, attracted his attention. One moment's look, and they recognised each other. They continued to hold secret communications. Champa Dal heard everything, including the story of her vow, the period of which was to terminate the following day. It is customary, on the fulfilment of a vow, for some learned Brahman to make public recitations of events connected with the vow and the person who makes it. It was settled that Champa Dal should take upon himself the functions of the reciter. Accordingly, next morning, when it was proclaimed by beat of drum that the king wanted a learned Brahman who could recite the story of Keshavati on the fulfilment of her vow, Champa Dal touched the drum and said that he would make the recitation. Next morning a gorgeous assembly was held in the courtyard of the palace under a huge canopy of silk. The old king, Sahasra Dal, all the courtiers and the learned Brahmans of the country, were present there. Keshavati was also there behind a screen that she might not be exposed to the rude gaze of the people. Champa Dal, the reciter, sitting on a dais, began the story of Keshavati, as we have related it, from the beginning, commencing with the words —"There was a poor and half-witted Brahman, etc." As he was going on with the story, the reciter every now and then asked Keshavati behind the screen whether the story was correct; to which question she as often replied, "Quite correct; go on, Brahman." During the recitation of the story the Rakshasi maid-servant grew pale, as she perceived that her real character was discovered; and Sahasra Dal was astonished at the knowledge of the reciter regarding the history of his own life. The moment the story was finished, Sahasra Dal jumped up from his seat, and embracing the reciter, said, "You can be none other than my brother Champa Dal." Then the prince, inflamed with rage, ordered the maid-servant into his presence. A large hole, as deep as the height of a man, was dug in the ground; the maid-servant was put into it in a standing posture; prickly thorn was heaped around her up to the crown of her head: in this wise was the maid-servant buried alive. After this Sahasra Dal and his princess, and Champa Dal and Keshavati, lived happily together many years.

Thus my story endeth,
The Natiya-thorn withereth, etc.

V

THE STORY OF SWET-BASANTA

THERE was a rich merchant who had an only son whom he loved passionately. He gave to his son whatever he wanted. His son wanted a beautiful house in the midst of a large garden. The house was built for him, and the grounds were laid out into a fine garden. One day as the merchant's son was walking in his garden, he put his hand into the nest of a small bird called *toontooni*, and found in it an egg, which he took and put in an almirah which was dug into the wall of his house. He closed the door of the almirah, and thought no more of the egg.

Though the merchant's son had a house of his own, he had no separate establishment; at any rate he kept no cook, for his mother used to send him regularly his breakfast and dinner every day. The egg which he deposited in the wall-almirah one day burst, and out of it came a beautiful infant, a girl. But the merchant's son knew nothing about it. He had forgotten everything about the egg, and the door of the wall-almirah had been kept closed, though not locked, ever since the day the egg was put there. The child grew up within the wall-almirah without the knowledge of the merchant's son or of any one else. When the child could walk, it had the curiosity one day to open the door ; and seeing some food on the floor (the breakfast of the merchant's son sent by his mother), it came out, and ate a little of it, and returned to its cell in the wall-almirah. As the mother of the merchant's son sent him always more than he could himself eat, he perceived no diminution in the quantity. The girl of the wall-almirah used every day to come out and eat a part of the food, and after eating used to return to her place in the almirah. But as the girl got older and older, she began to eat more and more ; hence the merchant's son began to perceive a diminution in the quantity of his food. Not dreaming of the existence of the wall-almirah girl, he wondered that his mother should send him such a small quantity of food. He sent word to his mother, complaining of the insufficiency of his meals, and of the slovenly manner in which the food was served up in the dish ; for the girl of the wall-almirah used to finger the rice, curry, and other articles of food, and as she always went in a hurry back into the almirah that she might not be perceived by any one, she had no time to put the rice and the other things into proper order after she had eaten part of them. The mother was astonished at her son's complaint, for she gave always a much larger quantity than she knew her son could consume, and the food was served up on

The Girl of the Wall-Almirah.

WARWICK GOBLE

a silver plate neatly by her own hand. But as her son repeated the same complaint day after day, she began to suspect foul play. She told her son to watch and see whether any one ate part of it unperceived. Accordingly, one day when the servant brought the breakfast and laid it in a clean place on the floor, the merchant's son, instead of going to bathe as it had hitherto been his custom, hid himself in a secret place and began to watch. In a few minutes he saw the door of the wall-almirah open ; a beautiful damsel of sweet sixteen stepped out of it, sat on the carpet spread before the breakfast, and began to eat. The merchant's son came out of his hiding-place, and the damsel could not escape. "Who are you, beautiful creature ? You do not seem to be earth-born. Are you one of the daughters of the gods ? " asked the merchant's son. The girl replied, "I do not know who I am. This I know, that one day I found myself in yonder almirah, and have been ever since living in it." The merchant's son thought it strange. He now remembered that sixteen years before he had put in the almirah an egg he had found in the nest of a *toontooni* bird. The uncommon beauty of the wall-almirah girl made a deep impression on the mind of the merchant's son, and he resolved in his mind to marry her. The girl no more went into the almirah, but lived in one of the rooms of the spacious house of the merchant's son.

The next day the merchant's son sent word to his mother to the effect that he would like to get married. His mother reproached herself for not having long before thought of her son's marriage, and sent a message to her son to the effect that she and his father would the next day send *ghataks*[1] to different countries to seek for a suitable bride. The merchant's son sent word that he had secured for himself a most lovable young lady, and that if his parents had no objections he would produce her before them. Accordingly the young lady of the wall-almirah was taken to the merchant's house; and the merchant and his wife were so struck with the matchless beauty, grace, and loveliness of the stranger, that, without asking any questions as to her birth, the nuptials were celebrated.

In course of time the merchant's son had two sons; the elder he named Swet and the younger Basanta. The old merchant died and so did his wife. Swet and Basanta grew up fine lads, and the elder was in due time married. Some time after Swet's marriage his mother, the wall-almirah lady, also died, and the widower lost no time in marrying a young and beautiful wife. As Swet's wife was older than his stepmother, she became the mistress of the house. The stepmother, like all stepmothers, hated Swet and Basanta with a perfect hatred; and the two ladies were naturally often at loggerheads with each other.

It so happened one day that a fisherman brought to the merchant (we shall no longer call him the merchant's son, as his father had died) a fish of

[1] Professional match-makers.

singular beauty. It was unlike any other fish that had been seen. The fish had marvellous qualities ascribed to it by the fisherman. If any one eats it, said he, when he laughs *maniks*[1] will drop from his mouth, and when he weeps pearls will drop from his eyes. The merchant, hearing of the wonderful properties of the fish, bought it at one thousand rupees, and put it into the hands of Swet's wife, who was the mistress of the house, strictly enjoining on her to cook it well and to give it to him alone to eat. The mistress, or house-mother, who had overheard the conversation between her father-in-law and the fisherman, secretly resolved in her mind to give the cooked fish to her husband and to his brother to eat, and to give to her father-in-law instead a frog daintily cooked. When she had finished cooking both the fish and the frog, she heard the noise of a squabble between her stepmother-in-law and her husband's brother. It appears that Basanta, who was but a lad yet, was passionately fond of pigeons, which he tamed. One of these pigeons had flown into the room of his stepmother, who had secreted it in her clothes. Basanta rushed into the room, and loudly demanded the pigeon. His stepmother denied any knowledge of the pigeon, on which the elder brother, Swet, forcibly took out the bird from her clothes and gave it to his brother. The stepmother cursed and swore, and added, "Wait, when the head of the house comes home I will make him shed the blood

[1] *Manik*, or rather *manikya*, is a fabulous precious stone of incredible value. It is found on the head of some species of snakes, and is equal in value to the wealth of seven kings.

of you both before I give him water to drink." Swet's wife called her husband and said to him, "My dearest lord, that woman is a most wicked woman, and has boundless influence over my father-in-law. She will make him do what she has threatened. Our life is in imminent danger. Let us first eat a little, and let us all three run away from this place." Swet forthwith called Basanta to him, and told him what he had heard from his wife. They resolved to run away before nightfall. The woman placed before her husband and his brother-in-law the fish of wonderful properties, and they ate of it heartily. The woman packed up all her jewels in a box. As there was only one horse, and it was of uncommon fleetness, the three sat upon it; Swet held the reins, the woman sat in the middle with the jewel-box in her lap, and Basanta brought up the rear.

The horse galloped with the utmost swiftness. They passed through many a plain and many a noted town, till after midnight they found themselves in a forest not far from the bank of a river. Here the most untoward event took place. Swet's wife began to feel the pains of child-birth. They dismounted, and in an hour or two Swet's wife gave birth to a son. What were the two brothers to do in this forest? A fire must be kindled to give heat both to the mother and the new-born baby. But where was the fire to be got? There were no human habitations visible. Still fire must be procured—and it was the month of December—or else both the mother and the baby

WARWICK GOBLE

"On a sudden an elephant gorgeously caparisoned shot across his path."

would certainly perish. Swet told Basanta to sit beside his wife, while he set out in the darkness of the night in search of fire.

Swet walked many a mile in darkness. Still he saw no human habitations. At last the genial light of Sukra[1] somewhat illumined his path, and he saw at a distance what seemed a large city. He was congratulating himself on his journey's end and on his being able to obtain fire for the benefit of his poor wife lying cold in the forest with the new-born babe, when on a sudden an elephant, gorgeously caparisoned, shot across his path, and gently taking him up by his trunk, placed him on the rich *howdah*[2] on its back. It then walked rapidly towards the city. Swet was quite taken aback. He did not understand the meaning of the elephant's action, and wondered what was in store for him. A crown was in store for him. In that kingdom, the chief city of which he was approaching, every morning a king was elected, for the king of the previous day was always found dead in the morning in the room of the queen. What caused the death of the king no one knew; neither did the queen herself (for every successive king took her to wife) know the cause. And the elephant who took hold of Swet was the king-maker. Early in the morning it went about, sometimes to distant places, and whosoever was brought on its back was acknowledged king by the people. The elephant majestically marched through the crowded

[1] Venus, the Morning Star.
[2] The seat on the back of an elephant.

streets of the city, amid the acclamations of the people, the meaning of which Swet did not understand, entered the palace, and placed him on the throne. He was proclaimed king amid the rejoicings of some and the lamentations of others. In the course of the day he heard of the strange fatality which overtook every night the elected king of those realms, but being possessed of great discretion and courage, he took every precaution to avert the dreadful catastrophe. Yet he hardly knew what expedients to adopt, as he was unacquainted with the nature of the danger. He resolved, however, upon two things, and these were, to go armed into the queen's bedchamber, and to sit up awake the whole night. The queen was young and of exquisite beauty, and so guileless and benevolent was the expression of her face that it was impossible from looking at her to suppose that she could use any foul means of taking away the life of her nightly consort. In the queen's chamber Swet spent a very agreeable evening ; as the night advanced the queen fell asleep, but Swet kept awake, and was on the alert, looking at every creek and corner of the room, and expecting every minute to be murdered. In the dead of night he perceived something like a thread coming out of the left nostril of the queen. The thread was so thin that it was almost invisible. As he watched it he found it several yards long, and yet it was coming out. When the whole of it had come out, it began to grow thick, and in a few minutes it assumed the form of a huge serpent. In a moment

Swet cut off the head of the serpent, the body of which wriggled violently. He sat quiet in the room, expecting other adventures. But nothing else happened. The queen slept longer than usual as she had been relieved of the huge snake which had made her stomach its den. Early next morning the ministers came expecting as usual to hear of the king's death ; but when the ladies of the bedchamber knocked at the door of the queen they were astonished to see Swet come out. It was then known to all the people how that every night a terrible snake issued from the queen's nostrils, how it devoured the king every night, and how it had at last been killed by the fortunate Swet. The whole country rejoiced in the prospect of a permanent king. It is a strange thing, nevertheless it is true, that Swet did not remember his poor wife with the new-born babe lying in the forest, nor his brother attending on her. With the possession of the throne he seemed to forget the whole of his past history.

Basanta, to whom his brother had entrusted his wife and child, sat watching for many a weary hour, expecting every moment to see Swet return with fire. The whole night passed away without his return. At sunrise he went to the bank of the river which was close by, and anxiously looked about for his brother, but in vain. Distressed beyond measure, he sat on the river side and wept. A boat was passing by in which a merchant was returning to his country. As the boat was not far from the shore the merchant saw Basanta weeping ;

and what struck the attention of the merchant was the heap of what looked like pearls near the weeping man. At the request of the merchant the boatman took his vessel towards the bank; the merchant went to the weeping man, and found that the heap was a heap of real pearls of the finest lustre: and what astonished him most of all was that the heap was increasing every second, for the tear-drops that were falling from his eyes fell to the ground not as tears but as pearls. The merchant stowed away the heap of pearls into his boat, and with the help of his servants caught hold of Basanta himself, put him on board the vessel, and tied him to a post. Basanta, of course, resisted; but what could he do against so many? Thinking of his brother, his brother's wife and baby, and his own captivity, Basanta wept more bitterly than before, which mightily pleased the merchant, as the more tears his captive shed the richer he himself became. When the merchant reached his native town he confined Basanta in a room, and at stated hours every day scourged him in order to make him shed tears, every one of which was converted into a bright pearl. The merchant one day said to his servants, "As the fellow is making me rich by his weeping, let us see what he gives me by laughing." Accordingly he began to tickle his captive, on which Basanta laughed, and as he laughed a great many *maniks* dropped from his mouth. After this poor Basanta was alternately whipped and tickled all the day and far into the night; and the merchant, in consequence, became the wealthiest man in the land. Leaving Basanta subjected to the alternate processes of castigation and titillation, let us attend to the fortunes of the poor wife of Swet, alone in the forest, with a child just born.

Swet's wife, apparently deserted by her husband and her brother-in-law, was overwhelmed with grief. A woman, but a few hours since delivered of a child—and her first child, alone, and in a forest, far from the habitations of men,—her case was indeed pitiable. She wept rivers of tears. Excessive grief, however, brought her relief. She fell asleep with the new-born baby in her arms. It so happened that at that hour the Kotwal (prefect of the police) of the country was passing that way. He had been very unfortunate with regard to his offspring; every child his wife presented him with died shortly after birth, and he was now going to bury the last infant on the banks of the river. As he was going, he saw in the forest a woman sleeping with a baby in her arms. It was a lively and beautiful boy. The Kotwal coveted the lovely infant. He quietly took it up, put in its place his own dead child, and returning home, told his wife that the child had not really died and had revived. Swet's wife, unconscious of the deceit practised upon her by the Kotwal, on waking found her child dead. The distress of her mind may be imagined. The whole world became dark to her. She was distracted with grief, and in her distraction she formed the resolution of committing suicide. The river was not far from the spot, and she determined to drown herself in it. She took in her hand the bundle of jewels and proceeded to the river-side. An old Brahman was at no great distance, performing his morning ablutions. He noticed the woman going into the water, and naturally thought that she was going to bathe; but when he saw her going far into deep waters, some suspicion arose in his mind. Discontinuing his devotions, he bawled out and ordered the woman to come to him. Swet's wife seeing that it was an old man that was calling her, retraced her steps and came to him. On being asked what she was about to do, she said that she was going to make an end of herself, and that as she had some jewels with her she would be obliged if he would accept them as a present. At the request of the old Brahman she related to him her whole story. The upshot was, that she was prevented from drowning herself, and that she was received into the Brahman's family, where she was treated by the Brahman's wife as her own daughter.

Years passed on. The reputed son of the Kotwal grew up a vigorous, robust lad. As the house of the old Brahman was not far from the Kotwal's, the Kotwal's son used accidentally to meet the handsome strange woman who passed for the Brahman's daughter. The lad liked the woman, and wanted to marry her. He spoke to his father about the woman, and the father spoke to the Brahman. The Brahman's rage knew no bounds. What! the infidel Kotwal's son aspiring to the hand of a Brahman's daughter! A dwarf may as well aspire to catch hold of the moon! But the Kotwal's son determined to have her by force. With this wicked object he one day scaled the wall that encompassed the Brahman's house, and got upon the thatched roof of the Brahman's cow-house. While he was reconnoitering from that lofty position, he heard the following conversation between two calves in the cow-house :—

First Calf. Men accuse us of brutish ignorance and immorality; but in my opinion men are fifty times worse.

Second Calf. What makes you say so, brother? Have you witnessed to-day any instance of human depravity?

First Calf. Who can be a greater monster of crime than the same lad who is at this moment standing on the thatched roof of this hut over our head?

Second Calf. Why, I thought it was only the son of our Kotwal; and I never heard that he was exceptionally vicious.

First Calf. You never heard, but now you hear from me. This wicked lad is now wishing to get married to his own mother!

The First Calf then related to the inquisitive Second Calf in full the story of Swet and Basanta; how they and Swet's wife fled from the vengeance of their stepmother; how Swet's wife was delivered of a child in the forest by the river-side ; how Swet was made king by the elephant, and how he succeeded in killing the serpent which issued out of the queen's nostrils ; how Basanta was carried away by the merchant, confined in a dungeon, and alternately flogged and tickled for pearls and *maniks ;* how the Kotwal exchanged his dead child for the living one of Swet ; how Swet's wife was prevented from drowning herself in the river by the Brahman ; how she was received into the Brahman's family and treated as his daughter ; how the Kotwal's son grew up a hardy, lusty youth, and fell in love with her ; and how at that very moment he was intent on accomplishing his brutal object. All this story the Kotwal's son heard from the thatched roof of the cow-house, and was struck with horror. He forthwith got down from the thatch, and went home and told his father that he must have an interview with the king. Notwithstanding his reputed father's protestations to the contrary, he had an interview with the king, to whom he repeated the whole story as he had overheard it from the thatch of the cow-house. The king now remembered his poor wife's case. She was brought from the house of the Brahman, whom he richly rewarded, and put her in her proper position as the queen of the kingdom ; the reputed son of the Kotwal was acknowledged as his own son, and proclaimed the heir-apparent to the throne ; Basanta was brought out of the dungeon, and the wicked merchant who had maltreated him was buried alive in the earth surrounded with thorns. After this, Swet, his wife and son, and Basanta, lived together happily for many years.

Now my story endeth,
The Natiya-thorn withereth, etc.

VI

THE EVIL EYE OF SANI

ONCE upon a time Sani, or Saturn, the god of bad luck, and Lakshmi, the goddess of good luck, fell out with each other in heaven. Sani said he was higher in rank than Lakshmi, and Lakshmi said she was higher in rank than Sani. As all the gods and goddesses of heaven were equally ranged on either side, the contending deities agreed to refer the matter to some human being who had a name for wisdom and justice. Now, there lived at that time upon earth a man of the name of Sribatsa,[1] who was as wise and just as he was rich. Him, therefore, both the god and the goddess chose as the settler of their dispute. One day, accordingly, Sribatsa was told that Sani and Lakshmi were wishing to pay him a visit to get their dispute settled. Sribatsa was in a fix. If he said Sani was higher in rank than Lakshmi, she would be angry with him and forsake him. If he said Lakshmi was higher in rank than Sani, Sani would cast his evil eye upon him. Hence he made up his mind

[1] *Sri* is another name of Lakshmi, and *batsa* means child; so that Sribatsa is literally the "child of fortune."

not to say anything directly, but to leave the god and the goddess to gather his opinion from his action. He got two stools made, the one of gold and the other of silver, and placed them beside him. When Sani and Lakshmi came to Sribatsa, he told Sani to sit upon the silver stool, and Lakshmi upon the gold stool. Sani became mad with rage, and said in an angry tone to Sribatsa, "Well, as you consider me lower in rank than Lakshmi, I will cast my eye on you for three years; and I should like to see how you fare at the end of that period." The god then went away in high dudgeon. Lakshmi, before going away, said to Sribatsa, "My child, do not fear. I'll befriend you." The god and the goddess then went away.

Sribatsa said to his wife, whose name was Chintamani, "Dearest, as the evil eye of Sani will be upon me at once, I had better go away from the house; for if I remain in the house with you, evil will befall you and me; but if I go away, it will overtake me only." Chintamani said, "That cannot be; wherever you go, I will go, your lot shall be my lot." The husband tried hard to persuade his wife to remain at home; but it was of no use. She would go with her husband. Sribatsa accordingly told his wife to make an opening in their mattress, and to stow away in it all the money and jewels they had. On the eve of leaving their house, Sribatsa invoked Lakshmi, who forthwith appeared. He then said to her, "Mother Lakshmi! as the evil eye of Sani is upon us, we are going away into exile; but do thou befriend us, and take care of our house and property." The goddess of good luck answered, "Do not fear; I'll befriend you; all will be right at last." They then set out on their journey. Sribatsa rolled up the mattress and put it on his head. They had not gone many miles when they saw a river before them. It was not fordable; but there was a canoe there with a man sitting in it. The travellers requested the ferryman to take them across. The ferryman said, "I can take only one at a time; but you are three—yourself, your wife, and the mattress." Sribatsa proposed that first his wife and the mattress should be taken across, and then he; but the ferryman would not hear of it. "Only one at a time," repeated he; "first let me take across the mattress." When the canoe with the mattress was in the middle of the stream, a fierce gale arose, and carried away the mattress, the canoe, and the ferryman, no one knows whither. And it was strange the stream also disappeared, for the place, where they saw a few minutes since the rush of waters, had now become firm ground. Sribatsa then knew that this was nothing but the evil eye of Sani.

Sribatsa and his wife, without a pice in their pocket, went to a village which was hard by. It was dwelt in for the most part by wood-cutters, who used to go at sunrise to the forest to cut wood, which they sold in a town not far from the village. Sribatsa proposed to the wood-cutters that he should go along with them to cut wood. They agreed. So he began to fell trees as well as

"They then set out on their journey."

WARWICK GOBLE

the best of them; but there was this difference between Sribatsa and the other wood-cutters, that whereas the latter cut any and every sort of wood, the former cut only precious wood like sandal-wood. The wood-cutters used to bring to market large loads of common wood, and Sribatsa only a few pieces of sandal-wood, for which he got a great deal more money than the others. As this was going on day after day, the wood-cutters through envy plotted together, and drove away from the village Sribatsa and his wife.

The next place they went to was a village of weavers, or rather cotton-spinners. Here Chintamani, the wife of Sribatsa, made herself useful by spinning cotton. And as she was an intelligent and skilful woman, she spun finer thread than the other women; and she got more money. This roused the envy of the native women of the village. But this was not all. Sribatsa, in order to gain the good grace of the weavers, asked them to a feast, the dishes of which were all cooked by his wife. As Chintamani excelled in cooking, the barbarous weavers of the village were quite charmed by the delicacies set before them. When the men went to their homes, they reproached their wives for not being able to cook so well as the wife of Sribatsa, and called them good-for-nothing women. This thing made the women of the village hate Chintamani the more. One day Chintamani went to the river-side to bathe along with the other women of the village. A boat had been lying on the bank stranded on the sand for many days; they had tried to move it, but in vain. It so happened that as Chintamani by accident touched the boat, it moved off to the river. The boatmen, astonished at the event, thought that the woman had uncommon power, and might be useful on similar occasions in future. They therefore caught hold of her, put her in the boat, and rowed off. The women of the village, who were present, did not offer any resistance as they hated Chintamani. When Sribatsa heard how his wife had been carried away by boatmen, he became mad with grief. He left the village, went to the river-side, and resolved to follow the course of the stream till he should meet the boat where his wife was a prisoner. He travelled on and on, along the side of the river, till it became dark. As there were no huts to be seen, he climbed into a tree for the night. Next morning as he got down from the tree he saw at the foot of it a cow called a Kapila-cow, which never calves, but which gives milk at all hours of the day whenever it is milked. Sribatsa milked the cow, and drank its milk to his heart's content. He was astonished to find that the cow-dung which lay on the ground was of a bright yellow colour; indeed, he found it was pure gold. While it was in a soft state he wrote his own name upon it, and when in the course of the day it became hardened, it looked like a brick of gold—and so it was. As the tree grew on the river-side, and as the Kapila-cow came morning and evening to supply him with milk, Sribatsa resolved to stay there till he should meet the boat. In the meantime the gold-bricks were increasing in number every day, for the cow both morning and evening deposited there the precious article. He put the gold-bricks, upon all of which his name was engraved, one upon another in rows, so that from a distance they looked like a hillock of gold.

Leaving Sribatsa to arrange his gold-bricks under the tree on the river-side we must follow the fortunes of his wife. Chintamani was a woman of great beauty; and thinking that her beauty might be her ruin, she, when seized by the boatmen, offered to Lakshmi the following prayer—— "O Mother Lakshmi! have pity upon me. Thou hast made me beautiful, but now my beauty will undoubtedly prove my ruin by the loss of honour and chastity. I therefore beseech thee, gracious Mother, to make me ugly, and to cover my body with some loathsome disease, that the boatmen may not touch me." Lakshmi heard Chintamani's prayer; and in the twinkling of an eye, while she was in the arms of the boatmen, her naturally beautiful form was turned into a vile carcase. The boatmen, on putting her down in the boat, found her body covered with loathsome sores which were giving out a disgusting stench. They therefore threw her into the hold of the boat amongst the cargo, where they used morning and evening to send her a little boiled rice and some water. In that hold Chintamani had a miserable life of it; but she greatly preferred that misery to the loss of chastity. The boatmen went to some port, sold the cargo, and were returning to their country when the sight of what seemed a hillock of gold, not far from the river-side, attracted their attention. Sribatsa, whose eyes were ever directed towards the river, was delighted when he saw a boat turn towards the bank, as he fondly imagined his wife might be in it. The boatmen went to the hillock of gold, when Sribatsa said that the gold was his. They put all the gold-bricks on board their vessel, took Sribatsa prisoner, and put him into the hold not far from the woman covered with sores. They of course immediately recognised each other, in spite of the change Chintamani had undergone, but thought it prudent not to speak to each other. They communicated there ideas, therefore, by signs and gestures. Now, the boatmen were fond of playing at dice, and as Sribatsa appeared to them from his looks to be a respectable man, they always asked him to join in the game. As he was an expert player, he almost always won the game, on which the boatmen, envying his superior skill, threw him overboard. Chintamani had the presence of mind, at that moment, to throw into the water a pillow which she had for resting her head upon. Sribatsa took hold of the pillow, by means of which he floated down the stream till he was carried at nightfall to what seemed a garden on the water's edge. There he stuck among the trees, where he remained the whole night, wet and shivering. Now, the garden belonged to an old widow who was in former years the chief flower-supplier to the king of that country. Through some cause or other a blight seemed to have come over her garden, as almost all the trees and plants ceased flowering; she had therefore given up her place as the flower-supplier of the royal household. On the morning following the night on which Sribatsa had stuck among the trees, however, the old woman on getting up from her bed could scarcely believe her eyes when she saw the whole garden ablaze with flowers. There was not a single tree or plant which was not begemmed with flowers. Not understanding the cause of such a miraculous sight, she took a walk through the garden, and found on the river's brink, stuck among the trees, a man shivering and almost dying with cold. She brought him to her cottage, lighted a fire to give him warmth, and showed him every attention, as she ascribed the wonderful flowering of her trees to his presence. After making him as comfortable as she could, she ran to the king's palace, and told his chief servants that she was again in a position to supply the palace with flowers; so she was restored to her former office as the flower-woman of the royal household. Sribatsa, who stopped a few days with the woman, requested her to recommend him to one of the king's ministers for a berth. He was accordingly sent for to the palace, and as he was at once found to be a man of intelligence, the king's minister asked him what post he would like to have. Agreeably to his wish he was appointed collector of tolls on the river. While discharging his duties as river toll-gatherer, in the course of a few days he saw the very boat in which his wife was a prisoner. He detained the boat, and charged the boatmen with the theft of gold-bricks which he claimed as his own. At the mention of gold-bricks the king himself came to the river-side, and was astonished beyond measure to see bricks made of gold, every one of which had the inscription—SRIBATSA. At the same time Sribatsa rescued from the boatmen his wife, who, the moment she came out of the vessel, became as lovely as before. The king heard the story of Sribatsa's misfortunes from his lips, entertained him in a princely style for many days, and at last sent him and his wife to their own country with presents of horses and elephants. The evil eye of Sani was now turned away from Sribatsa, and he again became what he formerly was, the Child of Fortune.

Thus my story endeth,
The Natiya-thorn withereth, etc.

VII

THE BOY WHOM SEVEN MOTHERS SUCKLED

ONCE on a time there reigned a king who had seven queens. He was very sad, for the seven queens were all barren. A holy mendicant, however, one day told the king that in a certain forest there grew a tree, on a branch of which hung seven mangoes ; if the king himself plucked those mangoes and gave one to each of the queens they would all become mothers. So the king went to the forest, plucked the seven mangoes that grew upon one branch, and gave a mango to each of the queens to eat. In a short time the king's heart was filled with joy, as he heard that the seven queens were all with child.

One day the king was out hunting, when he saw a young lady of peerless beauty cross his path. He fell in love with her, brought her to his palace, and married her. This lady was, however, not a human being, but a Rakshasi ; but the king of course did not know it. The king became dotingly fond of her ; he did whatever she told him. She said one day to the king, "You say that you love me more than any one else. Let me see whether you really love me so. If you love me, make your seven other queens blind, and let them be killed." The king became very sad at the request of his best-beloved queen, the more so as the seven queens were all with child. But there was nothing for it but to comply with the Rakshasi-queen's request. The eyes of the seven queens were plucked out of their sockets, and the queens themselves were delivered up to the chief minister to be destroyed. But the chief minister was a merciful man. Instead of killing the seven queens he hid them in a cave which was on the side of a hill. In course of time the eldest of the seven queens gave birth to a child. "What shall I do with the child," said she, "now that we are blind and are dying for want of food? Let me kill the child, and let us all eat of its flesh." So saying she killed the infant, and gave to each of her sister-queens a part of the child to eat. The six ate their portion, but the seventh or youngest queen did not eat her share, but laid it beside her. In a few days the second queen also was delivered of a child, and she did with it as her eldest sister had done with hers. So did the third, the fourth, the fifth, and the sixth queen. At last the seventh queen gave birth to a son; but she, instead of following the example of her sister-queens, resolved to nurse the child. The other queens demanded their portions of the newly-born babe. She gave each of them the portion she had got of the six children which had been killed, and which she had not eaten but laid aside. The other queens at once perceived that their portions were dry, and could not therefore be the parts of the child just born. The seventh queen told them that she had made up her mind not to kill the child but to nurse it. The others were glad to hear this, and they all said that they would help her in nursing the child. So the child was suckled by seven mothers, and it became after some years the hardiest and strongest boy that ever lived.

In the meantime the Rakshasi-wife of the king was doing infinite mischief to the royal household and to the capital. What she ate at the royal table did not fill her capacious stomach. She therefore, in the darkness of night, gradually ate up all the members of the royal family, all the king's servants and attendants, all his horses, elephants, and cattle; till none remained in the palace except she herself and her royal consort. After that she used to go out in the evenings into the city and eat up a stray human being here and there. The king was left unattended by servants; there was no person left to cook for him, for no one would take his service. At last the boy who had been suckled by seven mothers, and who had now grown up to a stalwart youth, volunteered his services. He attended on the king, and took every care to prevent the queen from swallowing him up, for he went away home long before nightfall; and the Rakshasi-queen never seized her victims except at night. Hence the queen determined in some other way to get rid of the boy. As the boy always boasted that he was equal to any work, however hard, the queen told him that she was suffering from some disease which could be cured only by eating a certain species of melon, which was twelve cubits long, but the stone of which was thirteen cubits long, and that that fruit could be had only from her mother, who lived on the other side of the ocean. She gave him a letter of introduction to her mother, in which she requested her to devour the boy the moment he put the letter into her hands. The boy, suspecting foul play, tore up the letter and proceeded on his journey. The dauntless youth passed through many lands, and at last stood on the shore of the ocean, on the other side of which was the country of the Rakshasis. He then bawled as loud as he could, and said, "Granny ! granny ! come and save your daughter ; she is dangerously ill." An old Rakshasi on the other side of the ocean heard the words, crossed the ocean, came to the boy, and on hearing the message took the boy on her back and re-crossed the ocean. So the boy was in the country of the Rakshasis. The twelve-cubit melon with its thirteen-cubit stone was given to the boy at once, and he was told to perform the journey back. But the boy pleaded fatigue, and begged to be allowed to rest one day. To this the old Rakshasi consented. Observing a stout club and a rope hanging in the Rakshasi's room, the boy inquired what they were there for. She replied, "Child, by that club and rope I cross the ocean. If any one takes the club and the rope in his hands, and addresses them in the following magical words—

WARWICK GOBLE

"A monstrous bird comes out apparently from the palace."

"*O stout club! O strong rope!*
Take me at once to the other side,"

then immediately the club and rope will take him to the other side of the ocean." Observing a bird in a cage hanging in one corner of the room, the boy inquired what it was. The old Rakshasi replied, "It contains a secret, child, which must not be disclosed to mortals, and yet how can I hide it from my own grandchild? That bird, child, contains the life of your mother. If the bird is killed, your mother will at once die." Armed with these secrets, the boy went to bed that night. Next morning the old Rakshasi, together with all the other Rakshasis, went to distant countries for forage. The boy took down the cage from the ceiling, as well as the club and rope. Having well secured the bird, he addressed the club and rope thus—

"*O stout club! O strong rope!*
Take me at once to the other side."

In the twinkling of an eye the boy was put on this side the ocean. He then retraced his steps, came to the queen, and gave her, to her astonishment, the twelve-cubit melon with its thirteen-cubit stone; but the cage with the bird in it he kept carefully concealed.

In the course of time the people of the city came to the king and said, "A monstrous bird comes out apparently from the palace every evening, and seizes the passengers in the streets and swallows them up. This has been going on for so long a time that the city has become almost desolate." The king could not make out what this monstrous bird was. The king's servant, the boy, replied that he knew the monstrous bird, and that he would kill it provided the queen stood beside the king. By royal command the queen was made to stand beside the king. The boy then took the bird from the cage which he had brought from the other side of the ocean, on seeing which she fell into a fainting fit. Turning to the king the boy said, "Sire, you will soon perceive who the monstrous bird is that devours your subjects every evening. As I tear off each limb of this bird, the corresponding limb of the man-devourer will fall off." The boy then tore off one leg of the bird in his hand; immediately, to the astonishment of the whole assembly, for the citizens were all present, one of the legs of the queen fell off. And when the boy squeezed the throat of the bird, the queen gave up the ghost. The boy then related his own history and that of his mother and his stepmothers. The seven queens, whose eyesight was miraculously restored, were brought back to the palace; and the boy that was suckled by seven mothers was recognised by the king as his rightful heir. So they lived together happily.

Thus my story endeth,
The Natiya-thorn withereth, &c.

VIII

THE STORY OF PRINCE SOBUR

ONCE upon a time there lived a certain merchant who had seven daughters. One day the merchant put to his daughters the question: "By whose fortune do you get your living?" The eldest daughter answered—"Papa, I get my living by your fortune." The same answer was given by the second daughter, the third, the fourth, the fifth, and the sixth; but his youngest daughter said—"I get my living by my own fortune." The merchant got very angry with the youngest daughter, and said to her—"As you are so ungrateful as to say that you get your living by your own fortune, let me see how you fare alone. This very day you shall leave my house without a pice in your pocket." He forthwith called his palki-bearers, and ordered them to take away the girl and leave her in the midst of a forest. The girl begged hard to be allowed to take with her her work-box containing her needles and threads. She was allowed to do so. She then got into the palki, which the bearers lifted on their shoulders. The bearers had not gone many hundred yards to the tune of "Hoon! hoon! hoon! hoon! hoon! hoon!" when an old woman bawled out to them and bid them stop. On coming up to the palki, she said, "Where are you taking away my daughter?" for she was the nurse of the merchant's youngest child. The bearers replied, "The merchant has ordered us to take her away and leave her in the midst of a forest; and we are going to do his bidding." "I must go with her," said the old woman. "How will you be able to keep pace with us, as we must needs run?" said the bearers. "Anyhow I must go where my daughter goes," rejoined the old woman. The upshot was that, at the entreaty of the merchant's youngest daughter, the old woman was put inside the palki along with her. In the afternoon the palki-bearers reached a dense forest. They went far into it; and towards sunset they put down the girl and the old woman at the foot of a large tree, and retraced their steps homewards.

The case of the merchant's youngest daughter was truly pitiable. She was scarcely fourteen years old; she had been bred in the lap of luxury; and she was now here at sundown in the heart of what seemed an interminable forest, with not a penny in her pocket, and with no other protection than what could be given her by an old, decrepit, imbecile woman. The very trees of the forest looked upon her with pity. The gigantic tree, at whose foot she was mingling her tears with those of the old woman, said to her (for trees could speak in those days)—"Unhappy girl! I much pity you. In a short time the wild beasts of the forest will come out of their lairs and roam about for their prey ; and they are sure to devour you and your companion. But I can help you ; I will make an opening for you in my trunk. When you see the opening go into it ; I will then close it up ; and you will remain safe inside ; nor can the wild beasts touch you." In a moment the trunk of the tree was split into two. The merchant's daughter and the old woman went inside the hollow, on which the tree resumed its natural shape. When the shades of night darkened the forest the wild beasts came out of their lairs. The fierce tiger was there ; the wild bear was there ; the hard-skinned rhinoceros was there ; the bushy bear was there ; the musty elephant was there ; and the horned buffalo was there. They all growled round about the tree, for they got the scent of human blood. The merchant's daughter and the old woman heard from within the tree the growl of the beasts. The beasts came dashing against the tree ; they broke its branches ; they pierced its trunk with their horns ; they scratched its bark with their claws : but in vain. The merchant's daughter and her old nurse were safe within. Towards dawn the wild beasts went away. After sunrise the good tree said to her two inmates, "Unhappy women, the wild beasts have gone into their lairs after greatly tormenting me. The sun is up ; you can now come out." So saying the tree split itself into two, and the merchant's daughter and the old woman came out. They saw the extent of the mischief done by the wild beasts to the tree. Many of its branches had been broken down ; in many places the trunk had been pierced ; and in other places the bark had been stripped off. The merchant's daughter said to the tree, "Good mother, you are truly good to give us shelter at such a fearful cost. You must be in great pain from the torture to which the wild beasts subjected you last night." So saying she went to the tank which was near the tree, and bringing thence a quantity of mud, she besmeared the trunk with it, especially those parts which had been pierced and scratched. After she had done this, the tree said, "Thank you, my good girl, I am now greatly relieved of my pain. I am, however, concerned not so much about myself as about you both. You must be hungry, not having eaten the whole of yesterday. And what can I give you ? I have no fruit of my own to give you. Give to the old woman whatever money you have, and let her go into the city hard by and buy some food." They said they had no money. On searching, however, in the work-box she found five *cowries*.[1] The tree then told the old woman to go with the *cowries* to the city and buy some *khai*.[2] The old woman went to the city, which was not far, and said to one confectioner, "Please give me five *cowries'* worth of *khai*." The confectioner laughed at her and said, "Be off, you old hag, do you think *khai* can be had for five *cowries* ?" She tried another shop, and the shop-

[1] Shells used as money, one hundred and sixty of which could have been got a few years ago for one pice.

[2] Fried paddy.

WARWICK GOBLE

" Hundreds of peacocks of gorgeous plumes came to the embankments to eat the *khai*."

keeper, thinking the woman to be in great distress, compassionately gave her a large quantity of *khai* for the five *cowries*.

When the old woman returned with the *khai*, the tree said to the merchant's daughter, "Each of you eat a little of the *khai*, lay by more than half, and strew the rest on the embankments of the tank all round." They did as they were bidden, though they did not understand the reason why they were told to scatter the *khai* on the sides of the tank. They spent the day in bewailing their fate, and at night they were housed inside the trunk of the tree as on the previous night. The wild beasts came as before, further mutilated the tree, and tortured it as in the preceding night. But during the night a scene was being enacted on the embankments of the tank of which the two women saw the outcome only on the following morning. Hundreds of peacocks of gorgeous plumes came to the embankments to eat the *khai* which had been strewed on them; and as they strove with each other for the tempting food many of their plumes fell off their bodies. Early in the morning the tree told the two women to gather the plumes together, out of which the merchant's daughter made a beautiful fan. This fan was taken into the city to the palace, where the son of the king admired it greatly and paid for it a large sum of money. As each morning a quantity of plumes was collected, every day one fan was made and sold. So that in a short time the two women got rich. The tree then advised them to employ men in building a house for them to live in. Accordingly bricks were burnt, trees were cut down for beams and rafters, bricks were reduced to powder, lime was manufactured, and in a few months a stately, palace-like house was built for the merchant's daughter and her old nurse. It was thought advisable to lay out the adjoining grounds as a garden, and to dig a tank for supplying them with water.

In the meantime the merchant himself with his wife and six daughters had been frowned upon by the goddess of wealth. By a sudden stroke of misfortune he lost all his money, his house and property were sold, and he, his wife, and six daughters, were turned adrift penniless into the world. It so happened that they lived in a village not far from the place where the two strange women had built a palace and were digging a tank. As the once rich merchant was now supporting his family by the pittance which he obtained every day for his manual labour, he bethought himself of employing himself as a day labourer in digging the tank of the strange lady on the skirts of the forest. His wife said she would also go to dig the tank with him. So one day while the strange lady was amusing herself from the window of her palace with looking at the labourers digging her tank, to her utter surprise she saw her father and mother coming towards the palace, apparently to engage themselves as day labourers. Tears ran down her cheeks as she looked at them, for they were clothed in rags. She immediately sent servants to bring them inside the house. The poor man and woman were frightened beyond measure. They saw that the tank was all ready; and as it was customary in those days to offer a human sacrifice when the digging was over, they thought that they were called inside in order to be sacrificed. Their fears increased when they were told to throw away their rags and to put on fine clothes which were given to them. The strange lady of the palace, however, soon dispelled their fears; for she told them that she was their daughter, fell on their necks and wept. The rich daughter related her adventures, and the father felt she was right when she said that she lived upon her own fortune and not on that of her father. She gave her father a large fortune, which enabled him to go to the city in which he formerly lived, and to set himself up again as a merchant.

The merchant now bethought himself of going in his ship to distant countries for purposes of trade. All was ready. He got on board, ready to start, but, strange to say, the ship would not move. The merchant was at a loss what to make of this. At last the idea occurred to him that he had asked each of his six daughters, who were living with him, what thing she wished he should bring for her; but he had not asked that question of his seventh daughter who had made him rich. He therefore immediately despatched a messenger to his youngest daughter, asking her what she wished her father to bring for her on his return from his mercantile travels. When the messenger arrived she was engaged in her devotions, and hearing that a messenger had arrived from her father she said to him "Sobur," meaning "wait." The messenger understood that she wanted her father to bring for her something called *Sobur*. He returned to the merchant and told him that she wanted him to bring for her *Sobur*. The ship now moved of itself, and the merchant started on his travels. He visited many ports, and by selling his goods obtained immense profit. The things his six daughters wanted him to bring for them he easily got, but *Sobur*, the thing which he understood his youngest daughter wished to have, he could get nowhere. He asked at every port whether *Sobur* could be had there, but the merchants all told him that they had never heard of such an article of commerce. At the last port he went through the streets bawling out—"Wanted *Sobur*! wanted *Sobur*!" The cry attracted the notice of the son of the king of that country whose name was Sobur. The prince, hearing from the merchant that his daughter wanted *Sobur*, said that he had the article in question, and bringing out a small box of wood containing a magical fan with a looking-glass in it, said—"This is *Sobur* which your daughter wishes to have." The merchant having obtained the long-wished-for *Sobur* weighed anchor, and sailed for his native land. On his arrival he sent to his youngest daughter the said wonderful box. The daughter, thinking it to be a common wooden box, laid it aside. Some days after when she was at leisure she bethought herself of opening the box which her father had sent her. When she opened it she saw in it a beautiful fan, and in it a looking-glass. As she shook the fan, in a moment the Prince Sobur stood before her, and said—"You called me, here I am. What's your wish?" The merchant's daughter, astonished at the sudden appearance of a prince of such exquisite beauty, asked who he was, and how he had made his appearance there. The prince told her of the circumstances under which he gave the box to her father, and informed her of the secret that whenever the fan would be shaken he would make his appearance. The prince lived for a day or two in the house of the merchant's daughter, who entertained him hospitably. The upshot was, that they fell in love with each other, and vowed to each other to be husband and wife. The prince returned to his royal father and told him that he had selected a wife for himself. The day for the wedding was fixed. The merchant and his six daughters were invited. The nuptial knot was tied. But there was death in the marriage-bed. The six daughters of the merchant, envying the happy lot of their youngest sister, had determined to put an end to the life of her newly-wedded husband. They broke several bottles, reduced the broken pieces into fine powder, and scattered it profusely on the bed. The prince, suspecting no danger, laid himself down in the bed; but he had scarcely been there two minutes when he felt acute pain through his whole system, for the fine bottle-powder had gone through every pore of his body. As the prince became restless through pain, and was shrieking aloud, his attendants hastily took him away to his own country.

The king and queen, the parents of Prince Sobur, consulted all the physicians and surgeons of the kingdom; but in vain. The young prince was day and night screaming with pain, and no one could ascertain the disease, far less give him relief. The grief of the merchant's daughter may be imagined. The marriage knot had been scarcely tied when her husband was attacked, as she thought, by a terrible disease and carried away many hundreds of miles off. Though she had never seen her husband's country she determined to go there and nurse him. She put on the garb of a Sannyasi, and with a dagger in her hand set out on her journey. Of tender years, and unaccustomed to make long journeys on foot, she soon got weary and sat under a tree to rest. On the top of the tree was the nest of the divine bird Bihangama and his mate Bihangami. They were not in their nest at the time, but two of their young ones were in it. Suddenly the young ones on the top of the tree gave a scream which roused the half-drowsy merchant's daughter whom we shall now call the young Sannyasi. He saw near him a huge serpent raising its hood and about to climb into the tree. In a moment he cut the serpent into two, on which the young birds left off screaming. Shortly after the Bihangama and Bihangami came sailing through the air; and the latter said to the former—"I suppose our offspring as usual have been devoured by our great enemy the serpent. Ah me! I do not hear the cries of my young ones." On nearing the nest, however, they were agreeably surprised to find their offspring alive. The young ones told their dams how the young Sannyasi under the tree had destroyed the serpent. And sure enough the snake was lying there cut into two.

The Bihangami then said to her mate—"The young Sannyasi has saved our offspring from death, I wish we could do him some service in return." The Bihangama replied, "We shall presently do her service, for the person under the tree is not a man but a woman. She got married only last night to Prince Sobur, who, a few hours after, when jumping into his bed, had every pore of his body pierced with fine particles of ground bottles which had been spread over his bed by his envious sisters-in-law. He is still suffering pain in his native land, and, indeed, is at the point of death. And his heroic bride taking the garb of a Sannyasi is going to nurse him." "But," asked the Bihangami, "is there no cure for the prince?" "Yes, there is," replied the Bihangama: "if our dung which is lying on the ground round about, and which is hardened, be reduced to powder, and applied by means of a brush to the body of the prince after bathing him seven times with seven jars of water and seven jars of milk, Prince Sobur will undoubtedly get well." "But," asked the Bihangami, "how can the poor daughter of the merchant walk such a distance? It must take her many days, by which time the poor prince will have died." "I can," replied the Bihangama, "take the young lady on my back, and put her in the capital of Prince Sobur, and bring her back, provided she does not take any presents there." The merchant's daughter, in the garb of a Sannyasi, heard this conversation between the two birds, and begged the Bihangama to take her on his back. To this the bird readily consented. Before mounting on her aerial car she gathered a quantity of birds' dung and reduced it to fine powder. Armed with this potent drug she got up on the back of the kind bird, and sailing through the air with the rapidity of lightning, soon reached the capital of Prince Sobur. The young Sannyasi went up to the gate of the palace, and sent word to the king that he was acquainted with potent drugs and would cure the prince in a few hours. The king, who had tried all the best doctors in the kingdom without success, looked upon the Sannyasi as a mere pretender, but on the advice of his councillors agreed to give him a trial. The Sannyasi ordered seven jars of water and seven jars of milk to be brought to him. He poured the contents of all the jars on the body of the prince. He then applied, by means of a feather, the dung-powder he had already prepared to every pore of the prince's body. Thereafter seven jars of water and seven jars of milk were again six times poured upon him. When the prince's body was wiped, he felt perfectly well. The king ordered that the richest treasures he had should be presented to the wonderful doctor; but the Sannyasi refused to take any. He only wanted a ring from the prince's finger to preserve as a memorial. The ring was readily given him. The merchant's daughter hastened to the sea-shore where the Bihangama was awaiting her. In a moment they reached the tree of the divine birds. Hence the young bride walked to her house on the skirts of the forest. The following day she shook the magical fan, and forthwith Prince Sobur appeared before her. When the lady showed him the ring, he learnt with infinite surprise that his own wife was the doctor that cured him. The prince took away his bride to his palace in his far-off kingdom, forgave his sisters-in-law, lived happily for scores of years, and was blessed with children, grandchildren, and great-grandchildren.

Thus my story endeth,
The Natiya-thorn withereth, etc.

IX

THE ORIGIN OF OPIUM[1]

ONCE on a time there lived on the banks of the holy Ganga a Rishi,[2] who spent his days and nights in the performance of religious rites and in meditation upon God. From sunrise to sunset he sat on the river bank engaged in devotion, and at night he took shelter in a hut of palm-leaves which his own hand had raised in a bush hard by. There were no men and women for miles round. In the hut, however, there was a mouse, which used to live upon the leavings of the Rishi's supper. As it was not in the nature of the sage to hurt any living thing, our mouse never ran away from him, but, on the contrary, went to him, touched his feet, and played with him. The Rishi, partly in kindness to the little brute, and partly to have some one by to talk to at times, gave the mouse the power of speech. One night the mouse, standing on its hind-legs and joining together its fore-legs reverently,

[1] This story is not my own. It was recited to me by a story-teller of the other sex who rejoices in the *nom de plume* "An Inmate of the Calcutta Lunatic Asylum."

[2] A holy sage.

said to the Rishi, "Holy sage, you have been so kind as to give me the power to speak like men. If it will not displease your reverence, I have one more boon to ask." "What is it?" said the Rishi. "What is it, little mousie? Say what you want." The mouse answered—"When your reverence goes in the day to the river-side for devotion, a cat comes to the hut to catch me. And had it not been for fear of your reverence, the cat would have eaten me up long ago; and I fear it will eat me some day. My prayer is that I may be changed into a cat that I may prove a match for my foe." The Rishi became propitious to the mouse, and threw some holy water on its body, and it was at once changed into a cat.

Some nights after, the Rishi asked his pet, "Well, little puss, how do you like your present life?" "Not much, your reverence," answered the cat. "Why not?" demanded the sage. "Are you not strong enough to hold your own against all the cats in the world?" "Yes," rejoined the cat. "Your reverence has made me a strong cat, able to cope with all the cats in the world. But I do not now fear cats; I have got a new foe. Whenever your reverence goes to the river-side, a pack of dogs comes to the hut, and sets up such a loud barking that I am frightened out of my life. If your reverence will not be displeased with me, I beg you to change me into a dog." The Rishi said, "Be turned into a dog," and the cat forthwith became a dog.

Some days passed, when one night the dog

said thus to the Rishi: "I cannot thank your reverence enough for your kindness to me. I was but a poor mouse, and you not only gave me speech but turned me into a cat; and again you were kind enough to change me into a dog. As a dog, however, I suffer a great deal of trouble, I do not get enough food: my only food is the leavings of your supper, but that is not sufficient to fill the maw of such a large beast as you have made me. O how I envy those apes who jump about from tree to tree, and eat all sorts of delicious fruits! If your reverence will not get angry with me, I pray that I be changed into an ape." The kind-hearted sage readily granted his pet's wish, and the dog became an ape.

Our ape was at first wild with joy. He leaped from one tree to another, and sucked every luscious fruit he could find. But his joy was short-lived. Summer came on with its drought. As a monkey he found it hard to drink water out of a river or of a pool; and he saw the wild boars splashing in the water all the day long. He envied their lot, and exclaimed, "O how happy those boars are! All day their bodies are cooled and refreshed by water. I wish I were a boar." Accordingly at night he recounted to the Rishi the troubles of the life of an ape and the pleasures of that of a boar, and begged of him to change him into a boar. The sage, whose kindness knew no bounds, complied with his pet's request, and turned him into a wild boar. For two whole days our boar kept his body soaking wet, and on the third day, as he was splashing about in his favourite element, whom should he see but the king of the country riding on a richly caparisoned elephant. The king was out hunting, and it was only by a lucky chance that our boar escaped being bagged. He dwelt in his own mind on the dangers attending the life of a wild boar, and envied the lot of the stately elephant who was so fortunate as to carry about the king of the country on his back. He longed to be an elephant, and at night besought the Rishi to make him one.

Our elephant was roaming about in the wilderness, when he saw the king out hunting. The elephant went towards the king's suite with the view of being caught. The king, seeing the elephant at a distance, admired it on account of its beauty, and gave orders that it should be caught and tamed. Our elephant was easily caught, and taken into the royal stables, and was soon tamed. It so chanced that the queen expressed a wish to bathe in the waters of the holy Ganga. The king, who wished to accompany his royal consort, ordered that the newly-caught elephant should be brought to him. The king and queen mounted on his back. One would suppose that the elephant had now got his wishes, as the king had mounted on his back. But no. There was a fly in the ointment. The elephant, who looked upon himself as a lordly beast, could not brook the idea that a woman, though a queen, should ride on his back. He thought himself degraded. He jumped up so violently that both the king and queen fell to the ground. The king carefully picked up the queen, took her in his arms, asked her whether she had been much hurt, wiped off the dust from her clothes with his handkerchief, and tenderly kissed her a hundred times. Our elephant, after witnessing the king's caresses, scampered off to the woods as fast as his legs could carry him. As he ran he thought within himself thus : "After all, I see that a queen is the happiest of all creatures. Of what infinite regard is she the object ! The king lifted her up, took her in his arms, made many tender inquiries, wiped off the dust from her clothes with his own royal hands, and kissed her a hundred times ! O the happiness of being a queen ! I must tell the Rhisi to make me a queen !" So saying the elephant, after traversing the woods, went at sunset to the Rishi's hut, and fell prostrate on the ground at the feet of the holy sage. The Rishi said, "Well, what's the news ? Why have you left the king's stud ?" "What shall I say to your reverence ? You have been very kind to me ; you have granted every wish of mine. I have one more boon to ask, and it will be the last. By becoming an elephant I have got only my bulk increased, but not my happiness. I see that of all creatures a queen is the happiest in the world. Do, holy father, make me a queen." "Silly child," answered the Rishi, "how can I make you a queen ? Where can I get a kingdom for you, and a royal husband to boot ? All I can do is to change you into an exquisitely beautiful girl, possessed of charms to captivate the heart of a prince, if ever the gods grant you an interview with some great prince!" Our elephant agreed to the change; and in a moment the sagacious beast was transformed into a beautiful young lady, to whom the holy sage gave the name of Postomani, or the poppy-seed lady.

Postomani lived in the Rishi's hut, and spent her time in tending the flowers and watering the plants. One day, as she was sitting at the door of the hut during the Rishi's absence, she saw a man dressed in a very rich garb come towards the cottage. She stood up and asked the stranger who he was, and what he had come there for. The stranger answered that he had come a-hunting in those parts, that he had been chasing in vain a deer, that he felt thirsty, and that he came to the hut of the hermit for refreshment.

Postomani. Stranger, look upon this cot as your own house. I'll do everything I can to make you comfortable; I am only sorry we are too poor suitably to entertain a man of your rank, for if I mistake not you are the king of this country.

The king smiled. Postomani then brought out a water-pot, and made as if she would wash the feet of her royal guest with her own hands, when the king said, "Holy maid, do not touch my feet, for I am only a Kshatriya, and you are the daughter of a holy sage."

Postomani. Noble sir, I am not the daughter of the Rishi, neither am I a Brahmani girl; so there can be no harm in my touching your feet. Besides, you are my guest, and I am bound to wash your feet.

King. Forgive my impertinence. What caste do you belong to?

Postomani. I have heard from the sage that my parents were Kshatriyas.

King. May I ask you whether your father was a king, for your uncommon beauty and your stately demeanour show that you are a born princess.

Postomani, without answering the question, went inside the hut, brought out a tray of the most delicious fruits, and set it before the king. The king, however, would not touch the fruits till the maid had answered his questions. When pressed hard Postomani gave the following answer: "The holy sage says that my father was a king. Having been overcome in battle, he, along with my mother, fled into the woods. My poor father was eaten up by a tiger, and my mother at that time was brought to bed of me, and she closed her eyes as I opened mine. Strange to say, there was a bee-hive on the tree at the foot of which I lay; drops of honey fell into my mouth and kept alive the spark of life till the kind Rishi found me and brought me into his hut. This is the simple story of the wretched girl who now stands before the king."

King. Call not yourself wretched. You are the loveliest and most beautiful of women. You would adorn the palace of the mightiest sovereign.

The upshot was, that the king made love to the girl and they were joined in marriage by the Rishi. Postomani was treated as the favourite

"'You would adorn the palace of the mightiest sovereign.'"

WARWICK GOBLE

queen, and the former queen was in disgrace. Postomani's happiness, however, was short-lived. One day as she was standing by a well, she became giddy, fell into the water, and died. The Rishi then appeared before the king and said : "O king, grieve not over the past. What is fixed by fate must come to pass. The queen, who has just been drowned, was not of royal blood. She was born a mouse ; I then changed her successively, according to her own wish, into a cat, a dog, an ape, a boar, an elephant, and a beautiful girl. Now that she is gone, do you again take into favour your former queen. As for my reputed daughter, through the favour of the gods I'll make her name immortal. Let her body remain in the well ; fill the well up with earth. Out of her flesh and bones will grow a tree which shall be called after her Posto, that is, the Poppy tree. From this tree will be obtained a drug called opium, which will be celebrated as a powerful medicine through all ages, and which will always be either swallowed or smoked as a wonderful narcotic to the end of time. The opium swallower or smoker will have one quality of each of the animals to which Postomani was transformed. He will be mischievous like a mouse, fond of milk like a cat, quarrelsome like a dog, filthy like an ape, savage like a boar, and high-tempered like a queen."

Thus my story endeth,
The Natiya-thorn withereth, etc.

X

STRIKE BUT HEAR

ONCE upon a time there reigned a king who had three sons. His subjects one day came to him and said, "O incarnation of justice! the kingdom is infested with thieves and robbers. Our property is not safe. We pray your majesty to catch hold of these thieves and punish them." The king said to his sons, "O my sons, I am old, but you are all in the prime of manhood. How is it that my kingdom is full of thieves? I look to you to catch hold of these thieves." The three princes then made up their minds to patrol the city every night. With this view they set up a station in the outskirts of the city, where they kept their horses. In the early part of the night the eldest prince rode upon his horse and went through the whole city, but did not see a single thief. He came back to the station. About midnight the second prince got upon his horse and rode through every part of the city, but he did not see or hear of a single thief. He came also back to the station. Some hours after midnight the youngest

WARWICK GOBLE

"He saw a beautiful woman coming out of the palace."

prince went the rounds, and when he came near the gate of the palace where his father lived, he saw a beautiful woman coming out of the palace. The prince accosted the woman, and asked who she was and where she was going at that hour of the night. The woman answered, "I am Rajlakshmi,[1] the guardian deity of this palace. The king will be killed this night. I am therefore not needed here. I am going away." The prince did not know what to make of this message. After a moment's reflection he said to the goddess, "But suppose the king is not killed to-night, then have you any objection to return to the palace and stay there?" "I have no objection," replied the goddess. The prince then begged the goddess to go in, promising to do his best to prevent the king from being killed. Then the goddess entered the palace again, and in a moment went the prince knew not whither.

The prince went straight into the bedroom of his royal father. There he lay immersed in deep sleep. His second and young wife, the stepmother of our prince, was sleeping in another bed in the room. A light was burning dimly. What was his surprise when the prince saw a huge cobra going round and round the golden bedstead on which his father was sleeping. The prince with his sword cut the serpent in two. Not satisfied with killing the cobra, he cut it up into a hundred pieces, and put them inside the *pan* dish[2] which

[1] The tutelary goddess of a king's household.

[2] A vessel, made generally of brass, for keeping the *pan* leaf together with betel-nut and other spices.

was in the room. While the prince was cutting up the serpent a drop of blood fell on the breast of his stepmother who was sleeping hard by. The prince was in great distress. He said to himself, "I have saved my father but killed my mother." How was the drop of blood to be taken out of his mother's breast? He wrapped round his tongue a piece of cloth sevenfold, and with it licked up the drop of blood. But while he was in the act of doing this, his stepmother woke up, and opening her eyes saw that it was her stepson, the youngest prince. The young prince rushed out of the room. The queen, intending to ruin the youngest prince, whom she hated, called out to her husband, "My lord, my lord, are you awake? are you awake? Rouse yourself up. Here is a nice piece of business." The king on awaking inquired what the matter was. "The matter, my lord? Your worthy son, the youngest prince, of whom you speak so highly, was just here. I caught him in the act of touching my breast. Doubtless he came with a wicked intent. And this is your worthy son!" The king was horror-struck. The prince went to the station to his brothers, but told them nothing.

Early in the morning the king called his eldest son to him and said, "If a man to whom I intrust my honour and my life prove faithless, how should he be punished?" The eldest prince replied, "Doubtless such a man's head should be cut off; but before you kill, you should see whether the man is really faithless." "What do you mean ?" inquired the king. "Let your majesty be pleased to listen," answered the prince.

"Once on a time there lived a goldsmith who had a grown-up son. And this son had a wife who had the rare faculty of understanding the language of beasts ; but neither her husband nor any one else knew that she had this uncommon gift. One night she was lying in bed beside her husband in their house, which was close to a river, when she heard a jackal howl out, 'There goes a carcase floating on the river ; is there any one who will take off the diamond ring from the finger of the dead man and give me the corpse to eat ?' The woman understood the jackal's language, got up from bed and went to the river-side. The husband, who was not asleep, followed his wife at some distance so as not to be observed by her. The woman went into the water, tugged the floating corpse towards the shore, and saw the diamond ring on the finger. Unable to loosen it with her hand, as the fingers of the dead body had swelled, she bit it off with her teeth, and put the dead body upon land. She then went to her bed, whither she had been preceded by her husband. The young goldsmith lay beside his wife almost petrified with fear, for he concluded after what he saw that his wife was not a human being but a Rakshasi. He spent the rest of the night in tossing in his bed, and early in the morning spoke to his father in the following manner : 'Father, the woman whom thou hast given me to wife is not a real woman but a Rakshasi. Last night as I was lying in bed with her, I heard outside the house, towards the river-side, a jackal set up a fearful howl. On this she, thinking that I was asleep, got up from bed, opened the door, and went out to the river-side. Surprised to see her go out alone at the dead hour of night, I suspected evil and followed her, but so that she could not see me. What did she do, do you think? O horror of horrors! She went into the stream, dragged towards the shore the dead body of a man which was floating by, and began to eat it! I saw this with mine own eyes. I then returned home while she was feasting upon the carcase, and jumped into bed. In a few minutes she also returned, bolted the door, and lay beside me. O my father, how can I live with a Rakshasi? She will certainly kill me and eat me up one night.' The old goldsmith was not a little shocked to hear this account. Both father and son agreed that the woman should be taken into the forest and there left to be devoured by wild beasts. Accordingly the young goldsmith spoke to his wife thus: 'My dear love, you had better not cook much this morning; only boil rice and burn a brinjal, for I must take you to-day to see your father and mother, who are dying to see you.' At the mention of her father's house she became full of joy, and finished the cooking in no time. The husband and wife snatched a hasty breakfast and started on their journey. The way lay through a dense jungle, in which the goldsmith bethought himself of leaving his wife alone to be eaten up by wild beasts. But while they

WARWICK GOBLE

"'Husband, take up all this large quantity of gold and these precious stones.'"

were passing through this jungle the woman heard a serpent hiss, the meaning of which hissing, as understood by her, was as follows : 'O passer-by, how thankful should I be to you if you would catch hold of that croaking frog in yonder hole, which is full of gold and precious stones, and give me the frog to swallow, and you take the gold and precious stones.' The woman forthwith made for the frog, and began digging the hole with a stick. The young goldsmith was now quaking with fear, thinking his Rakshasi-wife was about to kill him. She called out to him and said, 'Husband, take up all this large quantity of gold and these precious stones.' The goldsmith, not knowing what to make of it, timidly went to the place, and to his infinite surprise saw the gold and the precious stones. They took up as much as they could. On the husband's asking his wife how she came to know of the existence of all this riches, she said that she understood the language of animals, and that the snake coiled up hard by had informed her of it. The goldsmith, on finding out what an accomplished wife he was blessed with, said to her, 'My love, it has got very late to-day ; it would be impossible to reach your father's house before nightfall, and we may be devoured by wild beasts in the jungle ; I propose therefore that we both return home.' It took them a long time to reach home, for they were laden with a large quantity of gold and precious stones. On coming near the house, the goldsmith said to his wife, 'My dear, you go by the back door, while I go by the front door and see my father in his shop and show him all this gold and these precious stones.' So she entered the house by the back door, and the moment she entered she was met by the old goldsmith, who had come that minute into the house for some purpose with a hammer in his hand. The old goldsmith, when he saw his Rakshasi daughter-in-law, concluded in his mind that she had killed and swallowed up his son. He therefore struck her on the head with the hammer, and she immediately died. That moment the son came into the house, but it was too late. Hence it is that I told your majesty that before you cut off a man's head you should inquire whether the man is really guilty."

The king then called his second son to him, and said, "If a man to whom I intrust my honour and my life prove faithless, how should he be punished?" The second prince replied, "Doubtless such a man's head should be cut off, but before you kill you should see whether the man is really faithless." "What do you mean?" inquired the king. "Let your majesty be pleased to listen," answered the prince.

"Once on a time there reigned a king who was very fond of going out a-hunting. Once while he was out hunting his horse took him into a dense forest far from his followers. He rode on and on, and did not see either villages or towns. He became very thirsty, but he could see neither pond, lake, nor stream. At last he found something dripping from the top of a tree. Concluding it to be rain-water which had rested in some cavity of the tree, he stood on horseback under the tree and caught the dripping contents in a small cup. It was, however, no rain-water. A huge cobra, which was on the top of the tree, was dashing in rage its fangs against the tree; and its poison was coming out and was falling in drops. The king, however, thought it was rain-water; though his horse knew better. When the cup was nearly filled with the liquid snake-poison, and the king was about to drink it off, the horse, to save the life of his royal master, so moved about that the cup fell from the king's hand and all the liquid spilled about. The king became very angry with his horse, and with his sword gave a cut to the horse's neck, and the horse died immediately. Hence it is that I told your majesty that before you cut off a man's head you should inquire whether the man is really guilty."

The king then called to him his third and youngest son, and said, "If a man to whom I intrust my honour and my life prove faithless, how should he be punished?" The youngest prince replied, "Doubtless such a man's head should be cut off, but before you kill you should see whether the man is really faithless." "What do you mean?" inquired the king. "Let your majesty be pleased to listen," answered the prince.

"Once on a time there reigned a king who had in his palace a remarkable bird of the Suka species. One day as the Suka went out to the fields for an airing, he saw his dad and dam, who pressed him to come and spend some days with them in their nest in some far-off land. The Suka answered he would be very happy to come, but he could not go without the king's leave ; he added that he would speak to the king that very day, and would be ready to go the following morning if his dad and dam would come to that very spot. The Suka spoke to the king, and the king gave leave with reluctance as he was very fond of the bird. So the next morning the Suka met his dad and dam at the place appointed, and went with them to his paternal nest on the top of some high tree in a far-off land. The three birds lived happily together for a fortnight, at the end of which period the Suka said to his dad and dam, 'My beloved parents, the king granted me leave only for a fortnight, and to-day the fortnight is over : to-morrow I must start for the city of the king.' His dad and dam readily agreed to the reasonable proposal, and told him to take a present to the king. After laying their heads together for some time they agreed that the present should be a fruit of the tree of Immortality. So early next morning the Suka plucked a fruit off the tree of Immortality, and carefully catching it in his beak, started on his aerial journey. As he had a heavy weight to carry, the Suka was not able to reach the city of the king that day, and was benighted on the road. He took shelter in a tree, and was at a loss to know where to keep the fruit. If he kept it in his beak it was sure, he thought, to fall out when he fell asleep. Fortunately he saw a hole in the trunk of the tree in which he had taken shelter, and accordingly put the fruit in it. It so happened that in that hole there was a snake; in the course of the night the snake darted its fangs on the fruit, and thus besmeared it with its poison. Early before crow-cawing the Suka, suspecting nothing, took up the fruit of Immortality in its beak, and began his aerial voyage. The Suka reached the palace while the king was sitting with his ministers. The king was delighted to see his pet bird come again, and greatly admired the beautiful fruit which the Suka had brought as a present. The fruit was very fair to look at; it was the loveliest fruit in all the earth; and as its name implies it makes the eater of it immortal. The king was going to eat it, but his courtiers said that it was not advisable for the king to eat it, as it might be a poisonous fruit. He accordingly threw it to a crow which was perched on the wall; the crow ate a part of it; but in a moment the crow fell down and died. The king, imagining that the Suka had intended to take away his life, took hold of the bird and killed it. The king ordered the stone of the deadly fruit, as it was thought to be, to be planted in a garden outside the city. The stone in course of time became a large tree bearing lovely fruit. The king ordered a fence to be put round the tree, and placed a guard lest people should eat of the fruit and die. There lived in that city an old Brahman and his wife, who used to live upon charity. The Brahman one day mourned his hard lot, and told his wife that instead of leading the wretched life of a beggar he would eat the fruit of the poisonous tree in the king's garden and thus end his days. So that very night he got up from his bed in order to get into the king's garden. His wife, suspecting her husband's intention, followed him, resolved also to eat of the fruit and die with her husband. As at that dead hour of night the guard was asleep, the old Brahman plucked a fruit and ate it. The woman said to her husband, 'If you die what is the use of my life? I'll also eat and die.' So saying she plucked a fruit and ate it. Thinking that the poison would take some time to produce its due effect, they both went home and lay in bed, supposing that they would never rise again. To their infinite surprise next morning they found themselves to be not only alive, but young and vigorous. Their neighbours could scarcely recognise them — they had become so changed. The old Brahman had become handsome and vigorous, no grey hairs, no wrinkles on his cheeks; and as for his wife, she had become as beautiful as any lady in the king's household. The king, hearing of this wonderful change, sent for the old Brahman, who told him all the circumstances. The king then greatly lamented the sad fate of his pet bird, and blamed himself for having killed it without fully inquiring into the case.

"Hence it is," continued the youngest prince, "that I told your majesty that before you cut off a man's head you should inquire whether the man is really guilty. I know your majesty thinks that last night I entered your chamber with wicked intent. Be pleased to hear me before you strike. Last night as I was on my rounds I saw a female figure come out of the palace. On challenging her she said that she was Rajlakshmi, the guardian deity of the palace ; and that she was leaving the palace as the king would be killed that night. I told her to come in, and that I would prevent the king from being killed. I went straight into your bedroom, and saw a large cobra going round and round your golden bedstead. I killed the cobra, cut it up into a hundred pieces, and put them in the *pan* dish. But while I was cutting up the snake, a drop of its blood fell on the breast of my mother ; and then I thought that while I had saved my father I had killed my mother. I wrapped round my tongue a piece of cloth sevenfold and licked up the drop of blood. While I was licking up the blood, my mother opened her eyes and noticed me. This is what I have done ; now cut off my head if your majesty wishes it."

The king filled with joy and gratitude embraced his son, and from that time loved him more even than he had loved him before.

Thus my story endeth,
The Natiya-thorn withereth, etc.

XI

THE ADVENTURES OF TWO THIEVES AND OF THEIR SONS

PART I

ONCE on a time there lived two thieves in a village who earned their livelihood by stealing. As they were well-known thieves, every act of theft in the village was ascribed to them whether they committed it or not; they therefore left the village, and, being resolved to support themselves by honest labour, went to a neighbouring town for service. Both of them were engaged by a householder; the one had to tend a cow, and the other to water a *champaka* plant. The elder thief began watering the plant early in the morning, and as he had been told to go on pouring water till some of it collected itself round the foot of the plant he went on pouring bucketful after bucketful: but to no purpose. No sooner was the water poured on the foot of the plant than it was forthwith sucked up by the thirsty earth; and it was late in the afternoon when the thief, tired with drawing water, laid himself down on the ground, and fell asleep. The younger thief fared no better. The cow which he had to tend was the most vicious in the whole country. When taken out of the village for pasturage it galloped away to a great distance with its tail erect; it ran from one paddy-field to another, and ate the corn and trod upon it; it entered into sugar-cane plantations and destroyed the sweet cane;—for all which damage and acts of trespass the neatherd was soundly rated by the owners of the fields. What with running after the cow from field to field, from pool to pool; what with the abusive language poured not only upon him, but upon his forefathers up to the fourteenth generation, by the owners of the fields in which the corn had been destroyed,—the younger thief had a miserable day of it. After a world of trouble he succeeded about sunset in catching hold of the cow, which he brought back to the house of his master. The elder thief had just roused himself from sleep when he saw the younger one bringing in the cow. Then the elder said to the younger—"Brother, why are you so late in coming from the fields?"

Younger. What shall I say, brother? I took the cow to that part of the meadow where there is a tank, near which there is a large tree. I let the cow loose, and it began to graze about without giving the least trouble. I spread my *gamchha*[1] upon the grass under the tree; and there was such a delicious breeze that I soon fell asleep, and I did not wake till after sunset; and when I awoke I

[1] A towel used in bathing.

saw my good cow grazing contentedly at the distance of a few paces. But how did you fare, brother ?

Elder. Oh, as for me, I had a jolly time of it. I had poured only one bucketful of water on the plant, when a large quantity rested round it. So my work was done, and I had the whole day to myself. I laid myself down on the ground ; I meditated on the joys of this new mode of life ; I whistled ; I sang ; and at last fell asleep. And I am up only this moment.

When this talk was ended, the elder thief, believing that what the younger thief had said was true, thought that tending the cow was more comfortable than watering the plant ; and the younger thief, for the same reason, thought that watering the plant was more comfortable than tending the cow : each therefore resolved to exchange his own work for that of the other.

Elder. Well, brother, I have a wish to tend the cow. Suppose to-morrow you take my work, and I yours. Have you any objection ?

Younger. Not the slightest, brother. I shall be glad to take up your work, and you are quite welcome to take up mine. Only let me give you a bit of advice. I felt it rather uncomfortable to sleep nearly the whole of the day on the bare ground. If you take a *charpoy*[1] with you, you will have a merry time of it.

Early the following morning the elder thief went out with the cow to the fields, not forgetting

[1] A sort of bed made of rope, supported by posts of wood.

to take with him a *charpoy* for his ease and comfort; and the younger thief began watering the plant. The latter had thought that one bucketful, or at the outside two bucketfuls, of water would be enough. But what was his surprise when he found that even a hundred bucketfuls were not sufficient to saturate the ground around the roots of the plant. He was dead tired with drawing water. The sun was almost going down, and yet his work was not over. At last he gave it up through sheer weariness.

The elder thief in the fields was in no better case. He took the cow beside the tank which the younger thief had spoken of, put his *charpoy* under the large tree hard by, and then let the cow loose. As soon as the cow was let loose it went scampering about in the meadow, jumping over hedges and ditches, running through paddy-fields, and injuring sugar-cane plantations. The elder thief was not a little put about. He had to run about the whole day, and to be insulted by the people whose fields had been trespassed upon. But the worst of it was, that our thief had to run about the meadow with the *charpoy* on his head, for he could not put it anywhere for fear it should be taken away. When the other neatherds who were in the meadow saw the elder thief running about in breathless haste after the cow with the *charpoy* on his head, they clapped their hands and raised shouts of derision. The poor fellow, hungry and angry, bitterly repented of the exchange he had made. After infinite trouble, and with the help of the other neatherds, he at last caught hold of the precious cow, and brought it home long after the village lamps had been lit.

When the two thieves met in the house of their master, they merely laughed at each other without speaking a word. Their dinner over, they laid themselves to rest, when there took place the following conversation :—

Younger. Well, how did you fare, brother ?

Elder. Just as you fared, and perhaps some degrees better.

Younger. I am of opinion that our former trade of thieving was infinitely preferable to this sort of honest labour, as people call it.

Elder. What doubt is there of that ? But, by the gods, I have never seen a cow which can be compared to this. It has no second in the world in point of viciousness.

Younger. A vicious cow is not a rare thing. I have seen some cows as vicious. But have you ever seen a plant like this *champaka* plant which you were told to water ? I wonder what becomes of all the water that is poured round about it. Is there a tank below its roots ?

Elder. I have a good mind to dig round it and see what is beneath it.

Younger. We had better do so this night when the good man of the house and his wife are asleep.

At about midnight the two thieves took spades and shovels and began digging round the plant. After digging a good deal the younger thief lighted upon some hard thing against which the shovel struck. The curiosity of both was excited. The younger thief saw that it was a large jar ; he thrust his hand into it and found that it was full of gold mohurs. But he said to the elder thief—"Oh, it is nothing ; it is only a large stone." The elder thief, however, suspected that it was something else ; but he took care not to give vent to his suspicion. Both agreed to give up digging as they had found nothing ; and they went to sleep. An hour or two after, when the elder thief saw that the younger thief was asleep, he quietly got up and went to the spot which had been digged. He saw the jar filled with gold mohurs. Digging a little near it, he found another jar also filled with gold mohurs. Overjoyed to find the treasure, he resolved to secure it. He took up both the jars, went to the tank which was near, and from which water used to be drawn for the plant, and buried them in the mud of its bank. He then returned to the house, and quietly laid himself down beside the younger thief, who was then fast asleep. The younger thief, who had first found the jar of gold mohurs, now woke, and softly stealing out of bed, went to secure the treasure he had seen. On going to the spot he did not see any jar ; he therefore naturally thought that his companion the elder thief had secreted it somewhere. He went to his sleeping partner, with a view to discover if possible by any marks on his body the place where the treasure had been hidden. He examined the person of his friend with the eye of a detective, and saw mud on his feet and near the ankles. He immediately concluded the treasure must have been concealed somewhere in the tank. But in what part of the tank? on which bank? His ingenuity did not forsake him here. He walked round all the four banks of the tank. When he walked round three sides, the frogs on them jumped into the water; but no frogs jumped from the fourth bank. He therefore concluded that the treasure must have been buried on the fourth bank. In a little he found the two jars filled with gold mohurs; he took them up, and going into the cow-house brought out the vicious cow he had tended, and put the two jars on its back. He left the house and started for his native village.

When the elder thief at crow-cawing got up from sleep, he was surprised not to find his companion beside him. He hastened to the tank and found that the jars were not there. He went to the cow-house, and did not see the vicious cow. He immediately concluded the younger thief must have run away with the treasure on the back of the cow. And where could he think of going? He must be going to his native village. No sooner did this process of reasoning pass through his mind than he resolved forthwith to set out and overtake the younger thief. As he passed through the town, he invested all the money he had in a costly pair of shoes covered with gold lace. He walked very fast, avoiding the public road and making short cuts. He descried the younger thief trudging on slowly with his cow. He went before him in the highway about a distance of 200 yards, and threw down on the road one shoe. He walked on another 200 yards and threw the other shoe at a place near which was a large tree; amid the thick leaves of that tree he hid himself. The younger thief coming along the public road saw the first shoe and said to himself—"What a beautiful shoe that is! It is of gold lace. It would have suited me in my present circumstances now that I have got rich. But what shall I do with one shoe?" So he passed on. In a short time he came to the place where the other shoe was lying. The younger thief said within himself—"Ah, here is the other shoe! What a fool I was, that I did not pick up the one I first saw! However it is not too late. I'll tie the cow to yonder tree and go for the other shoe." He tied the cow to the tree, and taking up the second shoe went for the first, lying at a distance of about 200 yards. In the meantime the elder thief got down from the tree, loosened the cow, and drove it towards his native village, avoiding the king's highway. The younger thief on returning to the tree found that the cow was gone. He of course concluded that it could have been done only by the elder thief. He walked as fast as his legs could carry him, and reached his native village long before the elder thief with the cow. He hid himself near the door of the elder thief's house. The moment the elder thief arrived with the cow, the younger thief accosted him, saying—"So you are come safe, brother. Let us go in and divide the money." To this proposal the elder thief readily agreed. In the inner yard of the house the two jars were taken down from the back of the cow; they went to a room, bolted the door, and began dividing. Two mohurs were taken up by the hand, one was put in one place, and the other in another; and they went on doing that till the jars became empty. But last of all one gold mohur remained. The question was—Who was to take it? Both agreed that it should be changed the next morning, and the silver cash equally divided. But with whom was the single mohur to remain? There was not a little wrangling about the matter. After a great deal of yea and nay, it was settled that it should remain with the elder thief, and that next morning it should be changed and equally divided.

At night the elder thief said to his wife and the other women of the house, "Look here, ladies, the younger thief will come to-morrow morning to demand the share of the remaining gold mohur; but I don't mean to give it to him. You do one thing to-morrow. Spread a cloth on the ground in the yard. I will lay myself on the cloth pretending to be dead; and to convince people that I am dead, put a *tulasi*[1] plant near my head. And when you see the younger thief coming to the door, you set up a loud cry and lamentation. Then he will of course go away, and I shall not have to pay his share of the gold mohur." To this proposal the women readily agreed. Accordingly the next day, about noon, the elder thief laid himself down

[1] The sacred basil.

in the yard like a corpse with the sacred basil near his head. When the younger thief was seen coming near the house, the women set up a loud cry, and when he came nearer and nearer, wondering what it all meant, they said, "Oh, where did you both go? What did you bring? What did you do to him? Look, he is dead!" So saying they rent the air with their cries. The younger thief, seeing through the whole, said, "Well, I am sorry my friend and brother is gone. I must now attend to his funeral. You all go away from this place, you are but women. I'll see to it that the remains are well burnt." He brought a quantity of straw and twisted it into a rope, which he fastened to the legs of the deceased man, and began tugging him, saying that he was going to take him to the place of burning. While the elder thief was being dragged through the streets, his body was getting dreadfully scratched and bruised, but he held his peace, being resolved to act his part out, and thus escape giving the share of the gold mohur. The sun had gone down when the younger thief with the corpse reached the place of burning. But as he was making preparations for a funeral pile, he remembered that he had not brought fire with him. If he went for fire leaving the elder thief behind, he would undoubtedly run away. What then was to be done? At last he tied the straw rope to the branch of a tree, and kept the pretended corpse hanging in the air, and he himself climbed into the tree and sat on that branch, keeping tight hold of the rope lest it should break, and the elder thief run away. While they were in this state, a gang of robbers passed by. On seeing the corpse hanging, the head of the gang said, "This raid of ours has begun very auspiciously. Brahmans and Pandits say that if on starting on a journey one sees a corpse, it is a good omen. Well, we have seen a corpse, it is therefore likely that we shall meet with success this night. If we do, I propose one thing: on our return let us first burn this dead body and then return home." All the robbers agreed to this proposal. The robbers then entered into the house of a rich man in the village, put its inmates to the sword, robbed it of all its treasures, and withal managed it so cleverly that not a mouse stirred in the village. As they were successful beyond measure, they resolved on their return to burn the dead body they had seen. When they came to the place of burning they found the corpse hanging as before, for the elder thief had not yet opened his mouth lest he should be obliged to give half of the gold mohur. The thieves dug a hollow in the ground, brought fuel, and laid it upon the hollow. They took down the corpse from the tree, and laid it upon the pile; and as they were going to set it on fire, the corpse gave out an unearthly scream and jumped up. That very moment the younger thief jumped down from the tree with a similar scream. The robbers were frightened beyond measure. They thought that a *Dana* (evil spirit) had possessed the corpse, and that a ghost jumped down from the tree. They ran away in great fear, leaving behind them the

"They ran away in great fear, leaving behind them the money and jewels."

WARWICK GOBLE

money and the jewels which they had obtained by robbery. The two thieves laughed heartily, took up all the riches of the robbers, went home, and lived merrily for a long time.

PART II

The elder thief and the younger thief had one son each. As they had been so far successful in life by practising the art of thieving, they resolved to train up their sons to the same profession. There was in the village a Professor of the Science of Roguery, who took pupils, and gave them lessons in that difficult science. The two thieves put their sons under this renowned Professor. The son of the elder thief distinguished himself very much, and bade fair to surpass his father in the art of stealing. The lad's cleverness was tested in the following manner. Not far from the Professor's house there lived a poor man in a hut, upon the thatch of which climbed a creeper of the gourd kind. In the middle of the thatch, which was also its topmost part, there was a splendid gourd, which the man and his wife watched day and night. They certainly slept at night, but then the thatch was so old and rickety that if even a mouse went up to it bits of straw and particles of earth used to fall inside the hut, and the man and his wife slept right below the spot where the gourd was; so that it was next to impossible to steal the gourd without the knowledge of its owners. The Professor said to his pupils—for he had many—

that any one who stole the gourd without being caught would be pronounced the dux of the school. Our elder thief's son at once accepted the offer. He said he would steal away the gourd if he were allowed the use of three things, namely, a string, a cat, and a knife. The Professor allowed him the use of these three things. Two or three hours after nightfall, the lad, furnished with the three things mentioned above, sat behind the thatch under the eaves, listening to the conversation carried on by the man and his wife lying in bed inside the hut. In a short time the conversation ceased. The lad then concluded that they must both have fallen asleep. He waited half an hour longer, and hearing no sound inside, gently climbed up on the thatch. Chips of straw and particles of earth fell upon the couple sleeping inside. The woman woke up, and rousing her husband said, "Look there, some one is stealing the gourd!" That moment the lad squeezed the throat of the cat, and puss immediately gave out her usual "Mew! mew! mew!" The husband said, "Don't you hear the cat mewing? There is no thief; it is only a cat." The lad in the meantime cut the gourd from the plant with his knife, and tied the string which he had with him to its stalk. But how was he to get down without being discovered and caught, especially as the man and the woman were now awake? The woman was not convinced that it was only a cat; the shaking of the thatch, and the constant falling of bits of straw and particles of dust, made her think that it was a human being that was upon the thatch. She was telling her husband to go out and see whether a man was not there; but he maintained that it was only a cat. While the man and woman were thus disputing with each other, the lad with great force threw down the cat upon the ground, on which the poor animal purred most vociferously; and the man said aloud to his wife, "There it is; you are now convinced that it was only a cat." In the meantime, during the confusion created by the clamour of the cat and the loud talk of the man, the lad quietly came down from the thatch with the gourd tied to the string. Next morning the lad produced the gourd before his teacher, and described to him and to his admiring comrades the manner in which he had committed the theft. The Professor was in ecstasy, and remarked, "The worthy son of a worthy father." But the elder thief, the father of our hopeful genius, was by no means satisfied that his son was as yet fit to enter the world. He wanted to prove him still further. Addressing his son he said, "My son, if you can do what I tell you, I'll think you fit to enter the world. If you can steal the gold chain of the queen of this country from her neck, and bring it to me, I'll think you fit to enter the world." The gifted son readily agreed to do the daring deed.

The young thief—for so we shall now call the son of the elder thief—made a reconnaissance of the palace in which the king and queen lived. He reconnoitred all the four gates, and all the outer and inner walls as far as he could; and gathered incidentally a good deal of information, from people living in the neighbourhood, regarding the habits of the king and queen, in what part of the palace they slept, what guards there were near the bedchamber, and who, if any, slept in the antechamber. Armed with all this knowledge the young thief fixed upon one dark night for doing the daring deed. He took with him a sword, a hammer and some large nails, and put on very dark clothes. Thus accoutred he went prowling about the Lion gate of the palace. Before the zenana[1] could be got at, four doors, including the Lion gate, had to be passed ; and each of these doors had a guard of sixteen stalwart men. The same men, however, did not remain all night at their post. As the king had an infinite number of soldiers at his command, the guards at the doors were relieved every hour ; so that once every hour at each door there were thirty-two men present, consisting of the relieving party and of the relieved. The young thief chose that particular moment of time for entering each of the four doors. At the time of relief when he saw the Lion gate crowded with thirty-two men, he joined the crowd without being taken notice of ; he then spent the hour preceding the next relief in the large open space and garden between two doors ; and he could not be taken notice of, as the night as well as his clothes was pitch dark.

[1] Zenana is not the name of a province in India, as the good people of Scotland the other day took it to be, but the innermost department of a Hindu or Mohammedan house which the women occupy.

In a similar manner he passed the second door, the third door, and the fourth door. And now the queen's bedchamber stared him in the face. It was in the third loft; there was a bright light in it; and a low voice was heard as that of a woman saying something in a humdrum manner. The young thief thought that the voice must be the voice of a maid-servant reciting a story, as he had learnt was the custom in the palace every night, for composing the king and queen to sleep. But how to get up into the third loft? The inner doors were all closed, and there were guards everywhere. But the young thief had with him nails and a hammer: why not drive the nails into the wall and climb up by them? True; but the driving of nails into the wall would make a great noise which would rouse the guards, and possibly the king and queen,—at any rate the maid-servant reciting stories would give the alarm. Our erratic genius had considered that matter well before engaging in the work. There is a water-clock in the palace which shows the hours; and at the end of every hour a very large Chinese gong is struck, the sound of which is so loud that it is not only heard all over the palace, but over most part of the city; and the peculiarity of the gong, as of every Chinese gong, was that nearly one minute must elapse after the first stroke before the second stroke could be made, to allow the gong to give out the whole of its sound. The thief fixed upon the minutes when the gong was struck at the end of every hour for driving nails into the wall. At ten o'clock when the gong was struck ten times, the thief found it easy to drive ten nails into the wall. When the gong stopped, the thief also stopped, and either sat or stood quiet on the ninth nail catching hold of the tenth which was above the other. At eleven o'clock he drove into the wall in a similar manner eleven nails, and got a little higher than the second story; and by twelve o'clock he was in the loft where the royal bedchamber was. Peeping in he saw a drowsy maid-servant drowsily reciting a story, and the king and queen apparently asleep. He went stealthily behind the story-telling maid-servant and took his seat. The queen was lying down on a richly furnished bedstead of gold beside the king. The massive chain of gold round the neck of the queen was gleaming in candle-light. The thief quietly listened to the story of the drowsy maid-servant. She was becoming more and more sleepy. She stopped for a second, nodded her head, and again resumed the story. It was plain she was under the influence of sleep. In a moment the thief cut off the head of the maid-servant with his sword, and himself went on reciting for some minutes the story which the woman was telling. The king and queen were unconscious of any change as to the person of the story-teller, for they were both in deep sleep. He stripped the murdered woman of her clothes, put them on himself, tied up his own clothes in a bundle, and walking softly, gently took off the chain from the neck of the queen. He then went through the rooms down stairs, ordered the inner guard to open the door, as she was obliged to go out of the palace for purposes of necessity. The guards, seeing that it was the queen's maid-servant, readily allowed her to go out. In the same manner, and with the same pretext, he got through the other doors, and at last out into the street. That very night, or rather morning, the young thief put into his father's hand the gold chain of the queen. The elder thief could scarcely believe his own eyes. It was so like a dream. His joy knew no bounds. Addressing his son he said—"Well done, my son; you are not only as clever as your father, but you have beaten me hollow. The gods give you long life, my son."

Next morning when the king and queen got up from bed, they were shocked to see the maid-servant lying in a pool of blood. The queen also found that her gold chain was not round her neck. They could not make out how all this could have taken place. How could any thief manage to elude the vigilance of so many guards? How could he get into the queen's bedchamber? And how could he again escape? The king found from the reports of the guards that a person calling herself the royal maid-servant had gone out of the palace some hours before dawn. All sorts of inquiries were made, but in vain. Proclamation was made in the city; a large reward was offered to any one who would give information tending to the apprehension of the thief and murderer. But no one responded to the call. At last the king ordered a camel to be brought to him. On the back of the animal was placed two large bags filled with gold mohurs. The man taking charge of the bags upon the camel was ordered to go through every part of the city making the following challenge :—" As the thief was daring enough to steal away a gold chain from the neck of the queen, let him further show his daring by stealing the gold mohurs from the back of this camel." Two days and nights the camel paraded through the city, but nothing happened. On the third night as the camel-driver was going his rounds he was accosted by a *sannyasi*,[1] who sat on a tiger's skin before a fire, and near whom was a monstrous pair of tongs. This *sannyasi* was no other than the young thief in disguise. The *sannyasi* said to the camel-driver—" Brother, why are you going through the city in this manner? Who is there so daring as to steal from the back of the king's camel? Come down, friend, and smoke with me." The camel-driver alighted, tied the camel to a tree on the spot, and began smoking. The mendicant supplied him not only with tobacco, but with *ganja* and other intoxicating drugs, so that in a short time the camel-driver became quite intoxicated and fell asleep. The young thief led away the camel with the treasure on its back in the dead of night, through narrow lanes and bye-paths to his own house. That very night the camel was killed, and its carcase buried in deep pits in the earth, and the thing was so

[1] A religious mendicant.

"The camel-driver alighted, tied the camel to a tree on the spot, and began smoking."

WARWICK GOBLE

managed that no one could discover any trace of it.

The next morning when the king heard that the camel-driver was lying drunk in the street, and that the camel had been made away with together with the treasure, he was almost beside himself with anger. Proclamation was made in the city to the effect that whoever caught the thief would get the reward of a lakh of rupees. The son of the younger thief—who, by the way, was in the same school of roguery with the son of the elder thief, though he did not distinguish himself so much—now came to the front and said that he would apprehend the thief. He of course suspected that the son of the elder thief must have done it—for who so daring and clever as he? In the evening of the following day the son of the younger thief disguised himself as a woman, and coming to that part of the town where the young thief lived, began to weep very much, and went from door to door saying—"O sirs, can any of you give me a bit of camel's flesh, for my son is dying, and the doctors say nothing but eating camel's meat can save his life. O for pity's sake, do give me a bit of camel's flesh." At last he went to the house of the young thief, and begged of the wife—for the young thief himself was out—to tell him where he could get hold of camel's flesh, as his son would assuredly perish if it could not be got. Saying this he rent the air with his cries, and fell down at the feet of the young thief's wife. Woman as she was, though the wife of a thief, she felt pity for the supposed woman, and said—"Wait, and I will try and get some camel's flesh for your son." So saying, she secretly went to the spot where the dead camel had been buried, brought a small quantity of flesh, and gave it to the party. The son of the younger thief was now entranced with joy. He went and told the king that he had succeeded in tracing the thief, and would be ready to deliver him up at night if the king would send some constables with him. At night the elder thief and his son were captured, the body of the camel dug out, and all the treasures in the house seized. The following morning the king sat in judgment. The son of the elder thief confessed that he had stolen the queen's gold chain, and killed the maid-servant, and had taken away the camel; but he added that the person who had detected him and his father—the younger thief—were also thieves and murderers, of which fact he gave undoubted proofs. As the king had promised to give a lakh of rupees to the detective, that sum was placed before the son of the younger thief. But soon after he ordered four pits to be dug in the earth in which were buried alive, with all sorts of thorns and thistles, the elder thief and the younger thief, and their two sons.

Here my story endeth,
The Natiya-thorn withereth, etc.

XII

THE GHOST-BRAHMAN

ONCE on a time there lived a poor Brahman, who not being a Kulin, found it the hardest thing in the world to get married. He went to rich people and begged of them to give him money that he might marry a wife. And a large sum of money was needed, not so much for the expenses of the wedding, as for giving to the parents of the bride. He begged from door to door, flattered many rich folk, and at last succeeded in scraping together the sum needed. The wedding took place in due time; and he brought home his wife to his mother. After a short time he said to his mother—"Mother, I have no means to support you and my wife; I must therefore go to distant countries to get money somehow or other. I may be away for years, for I won't return till I get a good sum. In the meantime I'll give you what I have; you make the best of it, and take care of my wife." The Brahman receiving his mother's blessing set out on his travels. In the evening of that very day, a ghost assuming the exact appearance of the Brahman came into the house.

The newly married woman, thinking it was her husband, said to him —" How is it that you have returned so soon? You said you might be away for years; why have you changed your mind?" The ghost said—" To-day is not a lucky day, I have therefore returned home; besides, I have already got some money." The mother did not doubt but that it was her son. So the ghost lived in the house as if he was its owner, and as if he was the son of the old woman and the husband of the young woman. As the ghost and the Brahman were exactly like each other in everything, like two peas, the people in the neighbourhood all thought that the ghost was the real Brahman. After some years the Brahman returned from his travels; and what was his surprise when he found another like him in the house. The ghost said to the Brahman—" Who are you? what business have you to come to my house?" "Who am I?" replied the Brahman, " let me ask who you are. This is my house; that is my mother, and this is my wife." The ghost said—" Why herein is a strange thing. Every one knows that this is my house, that is my wife, and yonder is my mother; and I have lived here for years. And you pretend this is your house, and that woman is your wife. Your head must have got turned, Brahman." So saying the ghost drove away the Brahman from his house. The Brahman became mute with wonder. He did not know what to do. At last he bethought himself of going to the king and of laying his case

"'How is it that you have returned so soon?'"

WARWICK GOBLE

before him. The king saw the ghost-Brahman as well as the Brahman, and the one was the picture of the other ; so he was in a fix, and did not know how to decide the quarrel. Day after day the Brahman went to the king and besought him to give him back his house, his wife, and his mother ; and the king, not knowing what to say every time, put him off to the following day. Every day the king tells him to—"Come to-morrow" ; and every day the Brahman goes away from the palace weeping and striking his forehead with the palm of his hand, and saying—"What a wicked world this is ! I am driven from my own house, and another fellow has taken possession of my house and of my wife ! And what a king this is ! He does not do justice."

Now, it came to pass that as the Brahman went away every day from the court outside the town, he passed a spot at which a great many cowboys used to play. They let the cows graze on the meadow, while they themselves met together under a large tree to play. And they played at royalty. One cowboy was elected king ; another, prime minister or vizier ; another, *kotwal*, or prefect of the police ; and others, constables. Every day for several days together they saw the Brahman passing by weeping. One day the cowboy king asked his vizier whether he knew why the Brahman wept every day. On the vizier not being able to answer the question, the cowboy king ordered one of his constables to bring the Brahman to him. One of them went and said to the Brahman—"The king requires your immediate attendance." The Brahman replied—"What for? I have just come from the king, and he put me off till to-morrow. Why does he want me again?" "It is our king that wants you—our neat-herd king," rejoined the constable. "Who is neat-herd king?" asked the Brahman. "Come and see," was the reply. The neat-herd king then asked the Brahman why he every day went away weeping. The Brahman then told him his sad story. The neat-herd king, after hearing the whole, said, "I understand your case; I will give you again all your rights. Only go to the king and ask his permission for me to decide your case." The Brahman went back to the king of the country, and begged his Majesty to send his case to the neat-herd king, who had offered to decide it. The king, whom the case had greatly puzzled, granted the permission sought. The following morning was fixed for the trial. The neat-herd king, who saw through the whole, brought with him next day a phial with a narrow neck. The Brahman and the ghost-Brahman both appeared at the bar. After a great deal of examination of witnesses and of speech-making, the neat-herd king said—"Well, I have heard enough. I'll decide the case at once. Here is this phial. Whichever of you will enter into it shall be declared by the court to be the rightful owner of the house the title of which is in dispute. Now, let me see, which of you will enter." The Brahman said—"You are a neat-herd, and your intellect is that of a neat-herd.

What man can enter into such a small phial?" "If you cannot enter," said the neat-herd king, "then you are not the rightful owner. What do you say, sir, to this?" turning to the ghost-Brahman and addressing him. "If you can enter into the phial, then the house and the wife and the mother become yours." "Of course I will enter," said the ghost. And true to his word, to the wonder of all, he made himself into a small creature like an insect, and entered into the phial. The neat-herd king forthwith corked up the phial, and the ghost could not get out. Then, addressing the Brahman, the neat-herd king said, "Throw this phial into the bottom of the sea, and take possession of your house, wife, and mother." The Brahman did so, and lived happily for many years and begat sons and daughters.

Here my story endeth,
The Natiya-thorn withereth, etc.

XIII

THE MAN WHO WISHED TO BE PERFECT

Once on a time a religious mendicant came to a king who had no issue, and said to him, "As you are anxious to have a son, I can give to the queen a drug, by swallowing which she will give birth to twin sons; but I will give the medicine on this condition, that of those twins you will give one to me, and keep the other yourself." The king thought the condition somewhat hard, but as he was anxious to have a son to bear his name, and inherit his wealth and kingdom, he at last agreed to the terms. Accordingly the queen swallowed the drug, and in due time gave birth to two sons. The twin brothers became one year old, two years old, three years old, four years old, five years old, and still the mendicant did not appear to claim his share; the king and queen therefore thought that the mendicant, who was old, was dead, and dismissed all fears from their minds. But the mendicant was not dead, but living; he was counting the years carefully. The young princes were put under tutors, and made rapid progress in learning, as well as in the arts of riding and shooting with the bow; and as they were uncommonly handsome, they were admired by all the people. When the princes were sixteen years old the mendicant made his appearance at the palace gate, and demanded the fulfilment of the king's promise. The hearts of the king and of the queen were dried up within them. They had thought that the mendicant was no more in the land of the living; but what was their surprise when they saw him standing at the gate in flesh and blood, and demanding one of the young princes for himself? The king and queen were plunged into a sea of grief. There was nothing for it, however, but to part with one of the princes; for the mendicant might by his curse turn into ashes not only both the princes, but also the king, queen, palace, and the whole of the kingdom to boot. But which one was to be given away? The one was as dear as the other. A fearful struggle arose in the hearts of the king and queen. As for the young princes, each of them said, "I'll go," "I'll go." The younger one said to the elder, "You are older, if only by a few minutes; you are the pride of my father; you remain at home, I'll go with the mendicant." The elder said to the younger, "You are younger than I am; you are the joy of my mother; you remain at home, I'll go with the mendicant." After a great deal of yea and nay, after a great deal of mourning and lamentation, after the queen had wetted her clothes with her tears, the elder prince was let go with the mendicant. But before the prince left his father's roof he planted with his own hands a tree in the courtyard of the palace, and said to his parents and brother, "This tree is my life. When you see the tree green and fresh, then know that it is well with me; when you see the tree fade in some parts, then know that I am in an ill case; and when you see the whole tree fade, then know that I am dead and gone." Then kissing and embracing the king and queen and his brother, he followed the mendicant.

As the mendicant and the prince were wending their way towards the forest they saw some dog's whelps on the roadside. One of the whelps said to its dam, "Mother, I wish to go with that handsome young man, who must be a prince." The dam said, "Go"; and the prince gladly took the puppy as his companion. They had not gone far when upon a tree on the roadside they saw a hawk and its young ones. One of the young ones said to its dam, "Mother, I wish to go with that handsome young man, who must be the son of a king." The hawk said, "Go"; and the prince gladly took the young hawk as his companion. So the mendicant, the prince, with the puppy and the young hawk, went on their journey. At last they went into the depth of the forest far away from the houses of men, where they stopped before a hut thatched with leaves. That was the mendicant's cell. The mendicant said to the prince, "You are to live in this hut with me. Your chief work will be to cull flowers from the forest for my devotions.

WARWICK GOBLE

"At dawn he used to cull flowers in the forest."

You can go on every side except the north. If you go towards the north evil will betide you. You can eat whatever fruit or root you like; and for your drink, you will get it from the brook." The prince disliked neither the place nor his work. At dawn he used to cull flowers in the forest and give them to the mendicant; after which the mendicant went away somewhere the whole day and did not return till sundown; so the prince had the whole day to himself. He used to walk about in the forest with his two companions—the puppy and the young hawk. He used to shoot arrows at the deer, of which there was a great number; and thus made the best of his time. One day as he pierced a stag with an arrow, the wounded stag ran towards the north, and the prince, not thinking of the mendicant's behest, followed the stag, which entered into a fine-looking house that stood close by. The prince entered, but instead of finding the deer he saw a young woman of matchless beauty sitting near the door with a dice-table set before her. The prince was rooted to the spot while he admired the heaven-born beauty of the lady. "Come in, stranger," said the lady; "chance has brought you here, but don't go away without having with me a game of dice." The prince gladly agreed to the proposal. As it was a game of risk they agreed that if the prince lost the game he should give his young hawk to the lady; and that if the lady lost it, she should give to the prince a young hawk just like that of the prince. The lady won the game; she therefore took the prince's young hawk and kept it in a hole covered with a plank. The prince offered to play a second time, and the lady agreeing to it, they fell to it again, on the condition that if the lady won the game she should take the prince's puppy, and if she lost it she should give to the prince a puppy just like that of the prince. The lady won again, and stowed away the puppy in another hole with a plank upon it. The prince offered to play a third time, and the wager was that, if the prince lost the game, he should give himself up to the lady to be done to by her anything she pleased; and that if he won, the lady should give him a young man exactly like himself. The lady won the game a third time; she therefore caught hold of the prince and put him in a hole covered over with a plank. Now, the beautiful lady was not a woman at all; she was a Rakshasi who lived upon human flesh, and her mouth watered at the sight of the tender body of the young prince. But as she had had her food that day she reserved the prince for the meal of the following day.

Meantime there was great weeping in the house of the prince's father. His brother used every day to look at the tree planted in the courtyard by his own hand. Hitherto he had found the leaves of a living green colour; but suddenly he found some leaves fading. He gave the alarm to the king and queen, and told them how the leaves were fading. They concluded that the life of the elder prince must be in great danger. The younger prince therefore resolved to go to the help of his brother, but before going he planted a tree in the courtyard of the palace, similar to the one his brother had planted, and which was to be the index of the manner of his life. He chose the swiftest steed in the king's stables, and galloped towards the forest. In the way he saw a dog with a puppy, and the puppy thinking that the rider was the same that had taken away his fellow-cub—for the two princes were exactly like each other—said, "As you have taken away my brother, take me also with you." The younger prince understanding that his brother had taken away a puppy, he took up that cub as a companion. Further on, a young hawk, which was perched on a tree on the roadside, said to the prince, "You have taken away my brother; take me also, I beseech you"; on which the younger prince readily took it up. With these companions he went into the heart of the forest, where he saw a hut which he supposed to be the mendicant's. But neither the mendicant nor his brother was there. Not knowing what to do or where to go, he dismounted from his horse, allowed it to graze, while he himself sat inside the house. At sunset the mendicant returned to his hut, and seeing the younger prince, said, "I am glad to see you. I told your brother never to go towards the north, for evil in that case would betide him; but it seems that, disobeying my orders, he has gone to the north and has fallen into the toils of a Rakshasi who lives there. There is no hope of rescuing him; perhaps he has already been devoured."

The younger prince forthwith went towards the north, where he saw a stag which he pierced with an arrow. The stag ran into a house which stood by, and the younger prince followed it. He was not a little astonished when, instead of seeing a stag, he saw a woman of exquisite beauty. He immediately concluded, from what he had heard from the mendicant, that the pretended woman was none other than the Rakshasi in whose power his brother was. The lady asked him to play a game of dice with her. He complied with the request, and on the same conditions on which the elder prince had played. The younger prince won ; on which the lady produced the young hawk from the hole and gave it to the prince. The joy of the two hawks on meeting each other was great. The lady and the prince played a second time, and the prince won again. The lady therefore brought to the prince the young puppy lying in the hole. They played a third time, and the prince won a third time. The lady demurred to producing a young man exactly like the prince, pretending that it was impossible to get one ; but on the prince insisting upon the fulfilment of the condition, his brother was produced. The joy of the two brothers on meeting each other was great. The Rakshasi said to the princes, "Don't kill me, and I will tell you a secret which will save the life of the elder prince." She then told them that the mendicant was a worshipper of the goddess Kali, who had a temple not far off; that he belonged to that sect of Hindus who seek perfection from intercourse with the spirits of departed men ; that he had already sacrificed at the altar of Kali six human victims whose skulls could be seen in niches inside her temple ; that he would become perfect when the seventh victim was sacrificed ; and that the elder prince was intended for the seventh victim. The Rakshasi then told the prince to go immediately to the temple to find out the truth of what she had said. To the temple they accordingly went. When the elder prince went inside the temple, the skulls in the niches laughed a ghastly laugh. Horror-struck at the sight and sound, he inquired the cause of the laughter ; and the skulls told him that they were glad because they were about to get another added to their number. One of the skulls, as spokesman of the rest, said, "Young prince, in a few days the mendicant's devotions will be completed, and you will be brought into this temple and your head will be cut off, and you will keep company with us. But there is one way by which you can escape that fate and do us good." "Oh, do tell me," said the prince, "what that way is, and I promise to do you all the good I can." The skull replied, "When the mendicant brings you into this temple to offer you up as a sacrifice, before cutting off your head he will tell you to prostrate yourself before Mother Kali, and while you prostrate yourself he will cut off your head. But take our advice, when he tells you to bow down before Kali, you tell him that as a prince you never bowed down to any one, that you never knew what bowing down was, and that the mendicant should show it to you by himself doing it in your presence. And when he bows down to show you how it is done, you take up your sword and separate his head from his body. And when you do that we shall all be restored to life, as the mendicant's vows will be unfulfilled." The elder prince thanked the skulls for their advice, and went into the hut of the mendicant along with his younger brother.

In the course of a few days the mendicant's devotions were completed. On the following day he told the prince to go along with him to the temple of Kali, for what reason he did not mention; but the prince knew it was to offer him up as a victim to the goddess. The younger prince also went with them, but he was not allowed to go inside the temple. The mendicant then stood in the presence of Kali and said to the prince, "Bow down to the goddess." The prince replied, "I have not, as a prince, bowed to any one; I do not know how to perform the act of prostration. Please show me the way first, and I'll gladly do it." The mendicant then prostrated himself before the goddess; and while he was doing so the prince at one stroke of his sword separated his head from his body. Immediately the skulls in the niches of the temple laughed aloud, and the goddess herself became propitious to the prince and gave him that virtue of perfection which the mendicant had sought to obtain. The skulls were again united to their respective bodies and became living men, and the two princes returned to their country.

Here my story endeth,
The Natiya-thorn withereth, etc.

XIV

A GHOSTLY WIFE

ONCE on a time there lived a Brahman who had married a wife, and who lived in the same house with his mother. Near his house was a tank, on the embankment of which stood a tree, on the boughs of which lived a ghost of the kind called *Sankchinni*.[1] One night the Brahman's wife had occasion to go to the tank, and as she went she brushed by a Sankchinni who stood near; on which the she-ghost got very angry with the woman, seized her by the throat, climbed into her tree, and thrust her into a hole in the trunk. There the woman lay almost dead with fear. The ghost put on the clothes of the woman and went into the house of the Brahman. Neither the Brahman nor his mother had any inkling of the change. The Brahman thought his wife returned from the tank, and the mother thought that it was her daughter-in-law. Next morning the mother-in-law discovered some change in her daughter-

[1] *Sankchinnis* or *Sankhachurnis* are female ghosts of white complexion. They usually stand at the dead of night at the foot of trees, and look like sheets of white cloth.

"The Brahman's wife had occasion to go to the tank, and as she went she brushed by a Sankchinni."

in-law. Her daughter-in-law, she knew, was constitutionally weak and languid, and took a long time to do the work of the house. But she had apparently become quite a different person. All of a sudden she had become very active. She now did the work of the house in an incredibly short time. Suspecting nothing, the old woman said nothing either to her son or to her daughter-in-law ; on the contrary, she inly rejoiced that her daughter-in-law had turned over a new leaf. But her surprise became every day greater and greater. The cooking of the household was done in much less time than before. When the mother-in-law wanted the daughter-in-law to bring anything from the next room, it was brought in much less time than was required in walking from one room to the other. The ghost, instead of going inside the next room, would stretch a long arm—for ghosts can lengthen or shorten any limb of their bodies—from the door and get the thing. One day the old woman observed the ghost doing this. She ordered her to bring a vessel from some distance, and the ghost unconsciously stretched her hand to several yards' distance, and brought it in a trice. The old woman was struck with wonder at the sight. She said nothing to her, but spoke to her son. Both mother and son began to watch the ghost more narrowly. One day the old woman knew that there was no fire in the house, and she knew also that her daughter-in-law had not gone out of doors to get it ; and yet, strange to say, the hearth in the kitchen-room was quite in a blaze. She went in, and, to her infinite surprise, found that her daughter-in-law was not using any fuel for cooking, but had thrust into the oven her foot, which was blazing brightly. The old mother told her son what she had seen, and they both concluded that the young woman in the house was not his real wife but a she-ghost. The son witnessed those very acts of the ghost which his mother had seen. An *Ojha*[1] was therefore sent for. The exorcist came, and wanted in the first instance to ascertain whether the woman was a real woman or a ghost. For this purpose he lighted a piece of turmeric and set it below the nose of the supposed woman. Now this was an infallible test, as no ghost, whether male or female, can put up with the smell of burnt turmeric. The moment the lighted turmeric was taken near her, she screamed aloud and ran away from the room. It was now plain that she was either a ghost or a woman possessed by a ghost. The woman was caught hold of by main force and asked who she was. At first she refused to make any disclosures, on which the *Ojha* took up his slippers and began belabouring her with them. Then the ghost said with a strong nasal accent—for all ghosts speak through the nose—that she was a *Sankchinni*, that she lived on a tree by the side of the tank, that she had seized the young Brahmani and put her in the hollow of her tree because one night she had touched her, and that if any person went to the hole the woman would be

[1] An exorcist, one who drives away ghosts from possessed persons.

found. The woman was brought from the tree almost dead ; the ghost was again shoebeaten, after which process, on her declaring solemnly that she would not again do any harm to the Brahman and his family, she was released from the spell of the *Ojha* and sent away ; and the wife of the Brahman recovered slowly. After which the Brahman and his wife lived many years happily together and begat many sons and daughters.

Thus my story endeth,
The Natiya-thorn withereth, etc.

XV

THE STORY OF A BRAHMADAITYA[1]

ONCE on a time there lived a poor Brahman who had a wife. As he had no means of livelihood, he used every day to beg from door to door, and thus got some rice which they boiled and ate, together with some greens which they gleaned from the fields. After some time it chanced that the village changed its owner, and the Brahman bethought himself of asking some boon of the new laird. So one morning the Brahman went to the laird's house to pay him court. It so happened that at that time the laird was making inquiries of his servants about the village and its various parts. The laird was told that a certain banyan-tree in the outskirts of the village was haunted by a number of ghosts; and that no man had ever the boldness to go to that tree at night. In bygone days some rash fellows went to the tree at night, but the necks of them all were wrung, and they all died. Since that time no man had ventured to go to the tree at night, though in the day some neat-

[1] The ghost of a Brahman who dies unmarried.

herds took their cows to the spot. The new laird on hearing this said, that if any one would go at night to the tree, cut one of its branches and bring it to him, he would make him a present of a hundred *bighas*[1] of rent-free land. None of the servants of the laird accepted the challenge, as they were sure they would be throttled by the ghosts. The Brahman, who was sitting there, thought within himself thus—"I am almost starved to death now, as I never get my bellyful. If I go to the tree at night and succeed in cutting off one of its branches I shall get one hundred *bighas* of rent-free land, and become independent for life. If the ghosts kill me, my case will not be worse, for to die of hunger is no better than to be killed by ghosts." He then offered to go to the tree and cut off a branch that night. The laird renewed his promise, and said to the Brahman that if he succeeded in bringing one of the branches of that haunted tree at night he would certainly give him one hundred *bighas* of rent-free land.

In the course of the day when the people of the village heard of the laird's promise and of the Brahman's offer, they all pitied the poor man. They blamed him for his foolhardiness, as they were sure the ghosts would kill him, as they had killed so many before. His wife tried to dissuade him from the rash undertaking; but in vain. He said he would die in any case; but there was some chance of his escaping, and of thus becoming independent for life. Accordingly, one hour after

[1] A *bigha* is about the third part of an acre.

sundown, the Brahman set out. He went to the outskirts of the village without the slightest fear as far as a certain *vakula*-tree (Mimusops Elengi), from which the haunted tree was about one rope distant. But under the *vakula*-tree the Brahman's heart misgave him. He began to quake with fear, and the heaving of his heart was like the upward and downward motion of the paddy-husking pedal. The *vakula*-tree was the haunt of a Brahmadaitya, who, seeing the Brahman stop under the tree, spoke to him, and said, "Are you afraid, Brahman? Tell me what you wish to do, and I'll help you. I am a Brahmadaitya." The Brahman replied, "O blessed spirit, I wish to go to yonder banyan-tree, and cut off one of its branches for the zemindar, who has promised to give me one hundred *bighas* of rent-free land for it. But my courage is failing me. I shall thank you very much for helping me." The Brahmadaitya answered, "Certainly I'll help you, Brahman. Go on towards the tree, and I'll come with you." The Brahman, relying on the supernatural strength of his invisible patron, who is the object of the fear and reverence of common ghosts, fearlessly walked towards the haunted tree, on reaching which he began to cut a branch with the bill which was in his hand. But the moment the first stroke was given, a great many ghosts rushed towards the Brahman, who would have been torn to pieces but for the interference of the Brahmadaitya. The Brahmadaitya said in a commanding tone, "Ghosts, listen. This is a poor Brahman. He wishes to

"The moment the first stroke was given, a great many ghosts rushed towards the Brahman."

WARWICK GOBLE

get a branch of this tree which will be of great use to him. It is my will that you let him cut a branch." The ghosts, hearing the voice of the Brahmadaitya, replied, "Be it according to thy will, lord. At thy bidding we are ready to do anything. Let not the Brahman take the trouble of cutting; we ourselves will cut a branch for him." So saying, in the twinkling of an eye, the ghosts put into the hands of the Brahman a branch of the tree, with which he went as fast as his legs could carry him to the house of the zemindar. The zemindar and his people were not a little surprised to see the branch; but he said, "Well, I must see to-morrow whether this branch is a branch of the haunted tree or not; if it be, you will get the promised reward."

Next morning the zemindar himself went along with his servants to the haunted tree, and found to their infinite surprise that the branch in their hands was really a branch of that tree, as they saw the part from which it had been cut off. Being thus satisfied, the zemindar ordered a deed to be drawn up, by which he gave to the Brahman for ever one hundred *bighas* of rent-free land. Thus in one night the Brahman became a rich man.

It so happened that the fields, of which the Brahman became the owner, were covered with ripe paddy, ready for the sickle. But the Brahman had not the means to reap the golden harvest. He had not a pice in his pocket for paying the wages of the reapers. What was the Brahman to do? He went to his spirit-friend the

Brahmadaitya, and said, "Oh, Brahmadaitya, I am in great distress. Through your kindness I got the rent-free land all covered with ripe paddy. But I have not the means of cutting the paddy, as I am a poor man. What shall I do?" The kind Brahmadaitya answered, "Oh, Brahman, don't be troubled in your mind about the matter. I'll see to it that the paddy is not only cut, but that the corn is threshed and stored up in granaries, and the straw piled up in ricks. Only you do one thing. Borrow from men in the village one hundred sickles, and put them all at the foot of this tree at night. Prepare also the exact spot on which the grain and the straw are to be stored up."

The joy of the Brahman knew no bounds. He easily got a hundred sickles, as the husbandmen of the village, knowing that he had become rich, readily lent him what he wanted. At sunset he took the hundred sickles and put them beneath the *vakula*-tree. He also selected a spot of ground near his hut for his magazine of paddy and for his ricks of straw; and washed the spot with a solution of cow-dung and water. After making these preparations he went to sleep.

In the meantime, soon after nightfall, when the villagers had all retired to their houses, the Brahmadaitya called to him the ghosts of the haunted tree, who were one hundred in number, and said to them, "You must to-night do some work for the poor Brahman whom I am befriending. The hundred *bighas* of land which he has got from the zemindar are all covered with standing ripe corn. He has not the means to reap it. This night you all must do the work for him. Here are, you see, a hundred sickles; let each of you take a sickle in hand and come to the field I shall show him. There are a hundred of you. Let each ghost cut the paddy of one *bigha*, bring the sheaves on his back to the Brahman's house, thresh the corn, put the corn in one large granary, and pile up the straw in separate ricks. Now, don't lose time. You must do it all this very night." The hundred ghosts at once said to the Brahmadaitya, "We are ready to do whatever your lordship commands us." The Brahmadaitya showed the ghosts the Brahman's house, and the spot prepared for receiving the grain and the straw, and then took them to the Brahman's fields, all waving with the golden harvest. The ghosts at once fell to it. A ghost harvest-reaper is different from a human harvest-reaper. What a man cuts in a whole day, a ghost cuts in a minute. *Mash, mash, mash*, the sickles went round, and the long stalks of paddy fell to the ground. The reaping over, the ghosts took up the sheaves on their huge backs and carried them all to the Brahman's house. The ghosts then separated the grain from the straw, stored up the grain in one huge store-house, and piled up the straw in many a fantastic rick. It was full two hours before sunrise when the ghosts finished their work and retired to rest on their tree. No words can tell either the joy of the Brahman and his wife when early next morning they opened the door of their hut, or the surprise of the villagers, when they saw the huge granary and the fantastic ricks of straw. The villagers did not understand it. They at once ascribed it to the gods.

A few days after this the Brahman went to the *vakula*-tree, and said to the Brahmadaitya, "I have one more favour to ask of you, Brahmadaitya. As the gods have been very gracious to me, I wish to feed one thousand Brahmans; and I shall thank you for providing me with the materials of the feast." "With the greatest pleasure," said the polite Brahmadaitya; "I'll supply you with the requirements of a feast for a thousand Brahmans; only show me the cellars in which the provisions are to be stored away." The Brahman improvised a store-room. The day before the feast the store-room was overflowing with provisions. There were one hundred jars of *ghi* (clarified butter), one hill of flour, one hundred jars of sugar, one hundred jars of milk, curds, and congealed milk, and the other thousand and one things required in a great Brahmanical feast. The next morning one hundred Brahman pastrycooks were employed; the thousand Brahmans ate their fill; but the host, the Brahman of the story, did not eat. He thought he would eat with the Brahmadaitya. But the Brahmadaitya, who was present there though unseen, told him that he could not gratify him on that point, as by befriending the Brahman the Brahmadaitya's allotted period had come to an end, and the *pushpaka*[1] chariot had been sent to

[1] The chariot of Kuvera, the Hindu god of riches.

him from heaven. The Brahmadaitya, being released from his ghostly life, was taken up into heaven ; and the Brahman lived happily for many years, begetting sons and grandsons.

Here my story endeth,
The Natiya-thorn withereth, etc.

XVI

THE STORY OF A HIRAMAN[1]

THERE was a fowler who had a wife. The fowler's wife said to her husband one day, "My dear, I'll tell you the reason why we are always in want. It is because you sell every bird you catch by your rods, whereas if we sometimes eat some of the birds you catch, we are sure to have better luck. I propose therefore that whatever bird or birds you bag to-day we do not sell, but dress and eat." The fowler agreed to his wife's proposal, and went out a-bird-catching. He went about from wood to wood with his limed rods, accompanied by his wife, but in vain. Somehow or other they did not succeed in catching any bird till near sundown. But just as they were returning homewards they caught a beautiful hiraman. The fowler's wife, taking the bird in her hand and feeling it all over, said, "What a small bird this is! how much meat can it have? There is no use in killing it." The hiraman said, "Mother,

1 "*Hiraman* (from *harit*, green, and *mani*, a gem), the name of a beautiful species of parrot, a native of the Molucca Islands (*Psittacus sinensis*)."—CAREY'S *Dictionary of the Bengalee Language*, vol. ii. part iii. p. 1537.

do not kill me, but take me to the king, and you will get a large sum of money by selling me." The fowler and his wife were greatly taken aback on hearing the bird speak, and they asked the bird what price they should set upon it. The hiraman answered, "Leave that to me; take me to the king and offer me for sale; and when the king asks my price, say, 'The bird will tell its own price,' and then I'll mention a large sum." The fowler accordingly went the next day to the king's palace, and offered the bird for sale. The king, delighted with the beauty of the bird, asked the fowler what he would take for it. The fowler said, "O great king, the bird will tell its own price." "What! can the bird speak?" asked the king. "Yes, my lord; be pleased to ask the bird its price," replied the fowler. The king, half in jest and half in seriousness, said, "Well, hiraman, what is your price?" The hiraman answered, "Please your majesty, my price is ten thousand rupees. Do not think that the price is too high. Count out the money for the fowler, for I'll be of the greatest service to your majesty." "What service can you be of to me, hiraman?" asked the king. "Your majesty will see that in due time," replied the hiraman. The king, surprised beyond measure at hearing the hiraman talk, and talk so sensibly, took the bird, and ordered his treasurer to tell down the sum of ten thousand rupees to the fowler.

The king had six queens, but he was so taken up with the bird that he almost forgot that they lived; at any rate, his days and nights were spent in the company, not of the queens, but of the bird. The hiraman not only replied intelligently to every question the king put, but it recited to him the names of the three hundred and thirty millions of the gods of the Hindu pantheon, the hearing of which is always regarded as an act of piety. The queens felt that they were neglected by the king, became jealous of the bird, and determined to kill it. It was long before they got an opportunity, as the bird was the king's inseparable companion. One day the king went out a-hunting, and he was to be away from the palace for two days. The six queens determined to avail themselves of the opportunity and put an end to the life of the bird. They said to one another, "Let us go and ask the bird which of us is the ugliest in his estimation, and she whom he pronounces the ugliest shall strangle the bird." Thus resolved, they all went into the room where the bird was; but before the queens could put any questions the bird so sweetly and so piously recited the names of the gods and goddesses, that the hearts of them all were melted into tenderness, and they came away without accomplishing their purpose. The following day, however, their evil genius returned, and they called themselves a thousand fools for having been diverted from their purpose. They therefore determined to steel their hearts against all pity, and to kill the bird without delay. They all went into the room, and said to the bird, "O hiraman, you are a very wise bird, we hear, and your judgments are all right; will you please tell us which of us is the handsomest and which the ugliest?" The bird, knowing the evil design of the queens, said to them, "How can I answer your questions remaining in this cage? In order to pronounce a correct judgment I must look minutely on every limb of you all, both in front and behind. If you wish to know my opinion you must set me free." The women were at first afraid of setting the bird free lest it should fly away; but on second thoughts they set it free after shutting all the doors and windows of the room. The bird, on examining the room, saw that it had a water-passage through which it was possible to escape. When the question was repeated several times by the queens, the bird said, "The beauty of not one of you can be compared to the beauty of the little toe of the lady that lives beyond the seven oceans and the thirteen rivers." The queens, on hearing their beauty spoken of in such slighting terms, became exceedingly furious, and rushed towards the bird to tear it in pieces; but before they could get at it, it escaped through the water-passage, and took shelter in a wood-cutter's hut which was hard by.

The next day the king returned home from hunting, and not finding the hiraman on its perch became mad with grief. He asked the queens, and they told him that they knew nothing about it. The king wept day and night for the bird, as he loved it much. His ministers became afraid lest his reason should give way, for he used every hour of the day to weep, saying, "O my hiraman! O my hiraman! where art thou gone?" Proclamation was made by beat of drum throughout the kingdom to the effect that if any person could produce before the king his pet hiraman he would be rewarded with ten thousand rupees. The wood-cutter, rejoiced at the idea of becoming independent for life, produced the precious bird and obtained the reward. The king, on hearing from the parrot that the queens had attempted to kill it, became mad with rage. He ordered them to be driven away from the palace and put in a desert place without food. The king's order was obeyed, and it was rumoured after a few days that the poor queens were all devoured by wild beasts.

After some time the king said to the parrot, "Hiraman, you said to the queens that the beauty of none of them could be compared to the beauty of even the little toe of the lady who lives on the other side of the seven oceans and thirteen rivers. Do you know of any means by which I can get at that lady?"

Hiraman. Of course I do. I can take your majesty to the door of the palace in which that lady of peerless beauty lives; and if your majesty will abide by my counsel, I will undertake to put that lady into your arms.

King. I will do whatever you tell me. What do you wish me to do?

Hiraman. What is required is a *pakshiraj*.[1] If

[1] Winged horse, literally, the *king of birds*.

you can procure a horse of that species, you can ride upon it, and in no time we shall cross the seven oceans and thirteen rivers, and stand at the door of the lady's palace.

King. I have, as you know, a large stud of horses; we can now go and see if there are any *pakshirajes* amongst them.

The king and the hiraman went to the royal stables and examined all the horses. The hiraman passed by all the fine-looking horses and those of high mettle, and alighted upon a wretched-looking lean pony, and said, "Here is the horse I want. It is a horse of the genuine *pakshiraj* breed, but it must be fed full six months with the finest grain before it can answer our purpose." The king accordingly put that pony in a stable by itself and himself saw every day that it was fed with the finest grain that could be got in the kingdom. The pony rapidly improved in appearance, and at the end of six months the hiraman pronounced it fit for service. The parrot then told the king to order the royal silversmith to make some *khais* [1] of silver. A large quantity of silver *khais* was made in a short time. When about to start on their aërial journey the hiraman said to the king, "I have one request to make. Please whip the horse only once at starting. If you whip him more than once, we shall not be able to reach the palace, but stick mid-way. And when we return homewards after capturing the lady, you are also to whip the horse only once; if you whip him more than once,

[1] *Khai* is fried paddy.

we shall come only half the way and remain there." The king then got upon the *pakshiraj* with the hiraman and the silver *khais*, and gently whipped the animal once. The horse shot through the air with the speed of lightning, passed over many countries, kingdoms, and empires, crossed the oceans and thirteen rivers, and alighted in the evening at the gate of a beautiful palace.

Now, near the palace-gate there stood a lofty tree. The hiraman told the king to put the horse in the stable hard by, and then to climb into the tree and remain there concealed. The hiraman took the silver *khais*, and with its beak began dropping *khai* after *khai* from the foot of the tree, all through the corridors and passages, up to the door of the bedchamber of the lady of peerless beauty. After doing this, the hiraman perched upon the tree where the king was concealed. Some hours after midnight, the maid-servant of the lady, who slept in the same room with her, wishing to come out, opened the door and noticed the silver *khais* lying there. She took up a few of them, and not knowing what they were, showed them to her lady. The lady, admiring the little silver bullets, and wondering how they could have got there, came out of her room and began picking them up. She saw a regular stream of them apparently issuing from near the door of her room, and proceeding she knew not how far. She went on picking up in a basket the bright, shining *khais* all through the corridors and passages, till she came to the foot of the tree. No sooner did the lady of peerless beauty come to the foot of the tree than the king, agreeably to instructions previously given to him by the hiraman, alighted from the tree and caught hold of the lady. In a moment she was put upon the horse along with himself. At that moment the hiraman sat upon the shoulder of the king, the king gently whipped the horse once, and they all were whirled through the air with the speed of lightning. The king, wishing to reach home soon with the precious prize, and forgetful of the instructions of the hiraman, whipped the horse again ; on which the horse at once alighted on the outskirts of what seemed a dense forest. "What have you done, O king ?" shouted out the hiraman. "Did I not tell you not to whip the horse more than once ? You have whipped him twice, and we are done for. We may meet with our death here." But the thing was done, and it could not be helped. The *pakshiraj* became powerless ; and the party could not proceed homewards. They dismounted ; but they could not see anywhere the habitations of men. They ate some fruits and roots, and slept that night there upon the ground.

Next morning it so chanced that the king of that country came to that forest to hunt. As he was pursuing a stag, whom he had pierced with an arrow, he came across the king and the lady of peerless beauty. Struck with the matchless beauty of the lady, he wished to seize her. He whistled, and in a moment his attendants flocked around him. The lady was made a captive, and her lover, who had brought her from her house on the other side of the seven oceans and thirteen rivers, was not put to death, but his eyes were put out, and he was left alone in the forest—alone, and yet not alone, for the good hiraman was with him.

The lady of peerless beauty was taken into the king's palace, as well as the pony of her lover. The lady said to the king that he must not come near her for six months, in consequence of a vow which she had taken, and which would be completed in that period of time. She mentioned six months, as that period would be necessary for recruiting the constitution of the *pakshiraj*. As the lady professed to engage every day in religious ceremonies, in consequence of her vow, a separate house was assigned to her, where she took the *pakshiraj* and fed him with the choicest grain. But everything would be fruitless if the lady did not meet the hiraman. But how is she to get a sight of that bird? She adopted the following expedient. She ordered her servants to scatter on the roof of her house heaps of paddy, grain, and all sorts of pulse for the refreshment of birds. The consequence was, that thousands of the feathery race came to the roof to partake of the abundant feast. The lady was every day on the look out for her hiraman. The hiraman, meanwhile, was in great distress in the forest. He had to take care not only of himself, but of the now blinded king. He plucked some ripe fruits in the forest, and gave them to the king to eat, and he ate of them himself. This was the manner of hiraman's life. The other birds of the forest spoke thus to the parrot—

"O hiraman, you have a miserable life of it in this forest. Why don't you come with us to an abundant feast provided for us by a pious lady, who scatters many maunds of pulse on the roof of her house for the benefit of our race? We go there early in the morning and return in the evening, eating our fill along with thousands of other birds." The hiraman resolved to accompany them next morning, shrewdly suspecting more in the lady's charity to birds than the other birds thought there was in it. The hiraman saw the lady, and had a long chat with her about the health of the blinded king, the means of curing his blindness, and about her escape. The plan adopted was as follows: The pony would be ready for aerial flight in a short time—for a great part of the six months had already elapsed; and the king's blindness could be cured if the hiraman could procure from the chicks of the bihangama and bihangami birds, who had their nest on the tree at the gate of the lady's palace beyond the seven oceans and thirteen rivers, a quantity of their ordure, fresh and hot, and apply it to the eyeballs of the blinded king. The following morning the hiraman started on his errand of mercy, remained at night on the tree at the gate of the palace beyond the seven oceans and thirteen rivers, and early the next morning waited below the nest of the birds with a leaf on his beak, into which dropped the ordure of the chicks. That moment the hiraman flew across the oceans and rivers, came to the forest, and applied the precious balm to the sightless sockets of the king.

The king opened his eyes and saw. In a few days the *pakshiraj* was in proper trim. The lady escaped to the forest and took the king up ; and the lady, king, and hiraman all reached the king's capital safe and sound. The king and the lady were united together in wedlock. They lived many years together happily, and begat sons and daughters ; and the beautiful hiraman was always with them reciting the names of the three hundred and thirty millions of gods.

Here my story endeth,
The Natiya-thorn withereth, etc.

"The lady, king, and hiraman all reached the king's capital safe and sound."

WARWICK GOBLE

XVII

THE ORIGIN OF RUBIES

THERE was a certain king who died leaving four sons behind him with his queen. The queen was passionately fond of the youngest of the princes. She gave him the best robes, the best horses, the best food, and the best furniture. The other three princes became exceedingly jealous of their youngest brother, and conspiring against him and their mother, made them live in a separate house, and took possession of the estate. Owing to over-indulgence, the youngest prince had become very wilful. He never listened to any one, not even to his mother, but had his own way in everything. One day he went with his mother to bathe in the river. A large boat was riding there at anchor. None of the boatmen were in it. The prince went into the boat, and told his mother to come into it. His mother besought him to get down from the boat, as it did not belong to him. But the prince said, "No, mother, I am not coming down; I mean to go on a voyage, and if you wish to come with me, then delay not but come up at once, or I shall be off in a trice." The queen besought the prince to do no such thing, but to come down instantly. But the prince gave no heed to what she said, and began to take up the anchor. The queen went up into the boat in great haste ; and the moment she was on board the boat started, and falling into the current passed on swiftly like an arrow. The boat went on and on till it reached the sea. After it had gone many furlongs into the open sea, the boat came near a whirlpool, where the prince saw a great many rubies of monstrous size floating on the waters. Such large rubies no one had ever seen, each being in value equal to the wealth of seven kings. The prince caught hold of half a dozen of those rubies, and put them on board. His mother said, "Darling, don't take up those red balls ; they must belong to somebody who has been shipwrecked, and we may be taken up as thieves." At the repeated entreaties of his mother the prince threw them into the sea, keeping only one tied up in his clothes. The boat then drifted towards the coast, and the queen and the prince arrived at a certain port where they landed.

The port where they landed was not a small place ; it was a large city, the capital of a great king. Not far from the place, the queen and her son hired a hut where they lived. As the prince was yet a boy, he was fond of playing at marbles. When the children of the king came out to play on a lawn before the palace, our young prince joined them. He had no marbles, but he played with the ruby which he had in his possession. The ruby was so hard that it broke every taw against which it struck. The daughter of the king, who used to watch the games from a balcony of the palace, was astonished to see a brilliant red ball in the hand of the strange lad, and wanted to take possession of it. She told her father that a boy of the street had an uncommonly bright stone in his possession which she must have, or else she would starve herself to death. The king ordered his servants to bring to him the lad with the precious stone. When the boy was brought, the king wondered at the largeness and brilliancy of the ruby. He had never seen anything like it. He doubted whether any king of any country in the world possessed so great a treasure. He asked the lad where he had got it. The lad replied that he got it from the sea. The king offered a thousand rupees for the ruby, and the lad not knowing its value readily parted with it for that sum. He went with the money to his mother, who was not a little frightened, thinking that her son had stolen the money from some rich man's house. She became quiet, however, on being assured that the money was given to him by the king in exchange for the red ball which he had picked up in the sea.

The king's daughter, on getting the ruby, put it in her hair, and, standing before her pet parrot, said to the bird, "Oh, my darling parrot, don't I look very beautiful with this ruby in my hair?" The parrot replied, "Beautiful! you look quite hideous with it! What princess ever puts only one ruby in her hair? It would be somewhat feasible if you had two at least." Stung with shame at the reproach cast in her teeth by the parrot, the princess went into the grief-chamber of the palace, and would neither eat nor drink. The king was not a little concerned when he heard that his daughter had gone into the grief-chamber. He went to her, and asked her the cause of her grief. The princess told the king what her pet parrot had said, and added, "Father, if you do not procure for me another ruby like this, I'll put an end to my life by mine own hands." The king was overwhelmed with grief. Where was he to get another ruby like it? He doubted whether another like it could be found in the whole world. He ordered the lad who had sold the ruby to be brought into his presence. "Have you, young man," asked the king, "another ruby like the one you sold me?" The lad replied, "No, I have not got one. Why, do you want another? I can give you lots, if you wish to have them. They are to be found in a whirlpool in the sea, far, far away. I can go and fetch some for you." Amazed at the lad's reply, the king offered rich rewards for procuring only another ruby of the same sort.

The lad went home and said to his mother that he must go to sea again to fetch some rubies for the king. The woman was quite frightened at the idea, and begged him not to go. But the lad was resolved on going, and nothing could prevent him from carrying out his purpose. He accordingly

"'What princess ever puts only one ruby in her hair?'"

went alone on board that same vessel which had brought him and his mother, and set sail. He reached the whirlpool, from near which he had formerly picked up the rubies. This time, however, he determined to go to the exact spot whence the rubies were coming out. He went to the centre of the whirlpool, where he saw a gap reaching to the bottom of the ocean. He dived into it, leaving his boat to wheel round the whirlpool. When he reached the bottom of the ocean he saw there a beautiful palace. He went inside. In the central room of the palace there was the god Siva, with his eyes closed, and absorbed apparently in intense meditation. A few feet above Siva's head was a platform, on which lay a young lady of exquisite beauty. The prince went to the platform and saw that the head of the lady was separated from her body. Horrified at the sight, he did not know what to make of it. He saw a stream of blood trickling from the severed head, falling upon the matted head of Siva, and running into the ocean in the form of rubies. After a little two small rods, one of silver and one of gold, which were lying near the head of the lady, attracted his eyes. As he took up the rods in his hands, the golden rod accidentally fell upon the head, on which the head immediately joined itself to the body, and the lady got up. Astonished at the sight of a human being, the lady asked the prince who he was and how he had got there. After hearing the story of the prince's adventures, the lady said, "Unhappy young man, depart instantly from this place; for when Siva finishes his meditations he will turn you to ashes by a single glance of his eyes." The young man, however, would not go except in her company, as he was over head and ears in love with the beautiful lady. At last they both contrived to run away from the palace, and coming up to the surface of the ocean they climbed into the boat near the centre of the whirlpool, and sailed away towards land, having previously laden the vessel with a cargo of rubies. The wonder of the prince's mother at seeing the beautiful damsel may be well imagined. Early next morning the prince sent a basin full of big rubies, through a servant. The king was astonished beyond measure. His daughter, on getting the rubies, resolved on marrying the wonderful lad who had made a present of them to her. Though the prince had a wife, whom he had brought up from the depths of the ocean, he consented to have a second wife. They were accordingly married, and lived happily for years, begetting sons and daughters.

Here my story endeth,
The Natiya-thorn withereth, etc.

"Coming up to the surface they climbed into the boat."

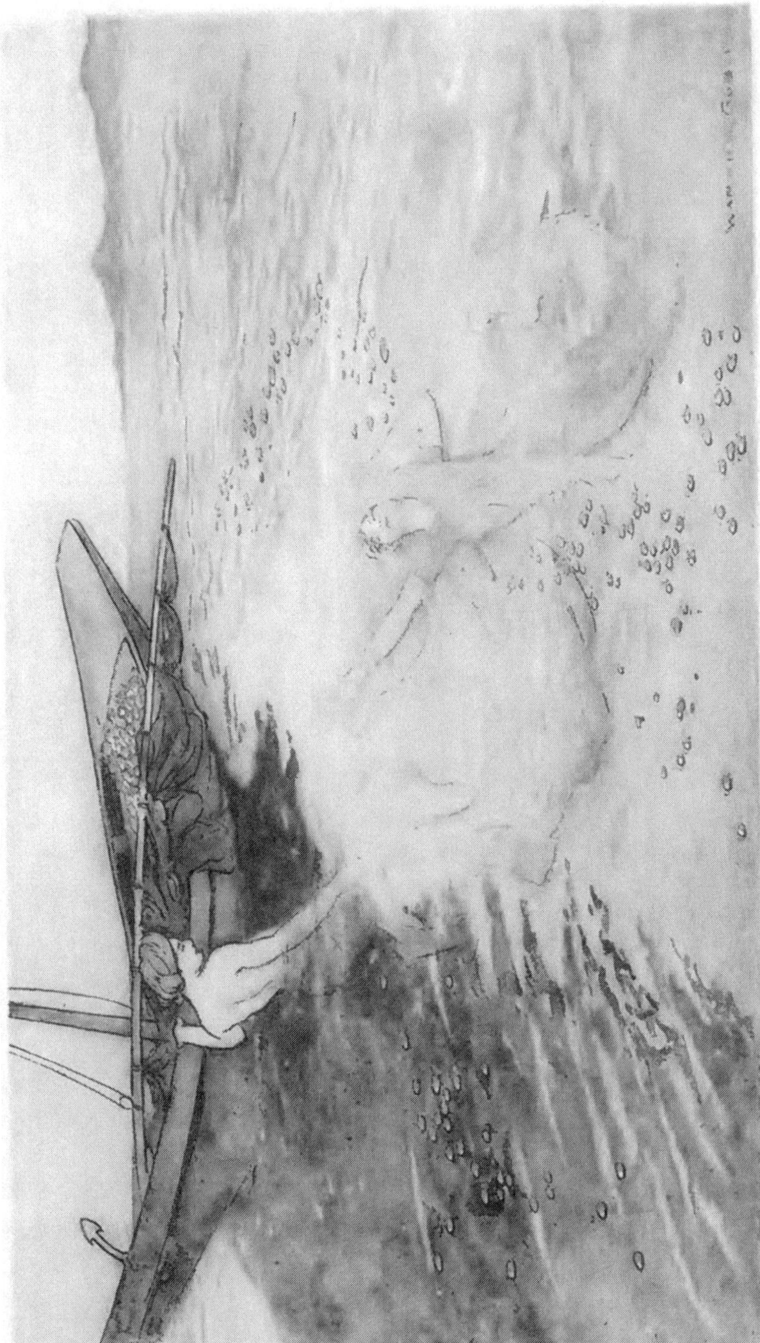

XVIII

THE MATCH-MAKING JACKAL

ONCE on a time there lived a weaver, whose ancestors were very rich, but whose father had wasted the property which he had inherited in riotous living. He was born in a palace-like house, but he now lived in a miserable hut. He had no one in the world, his parents and all his relatives having died. Hard by the hut was the lair of a jackal. The jackal, remembering the wealth and grandeur of the weaver's forefathers, had compassion on him, and one day coming to him, said, "Friend weaver, I see what a wretched life you are leading. I have a good mind to improve your condition. I'll try and marry you to the daughter of the king of this country." "I become the king's son-in-law!" replied the weaver; "that will take place only when the sun rises in the west." "You doubt my power?" rejoined the jackal; "you will see, I'll bring it about."

The next morning the jackal started for the king's city, which was many miles off. On the way he entered a plantation of the Piper betel plant, and plucked a large quantity of its leaves. He reached the capital, and contrived to get inside the palace. On the premises of the palace was a tank in which the ladies of the king's household performed their morning and afternoon ablutions. At the entrance of that tank the jackal laid himself down. The daughter of the king happened to come just at the time to bathe, accompanied by her maids. The princess was not a little struck at seeing the jackal lying down at the entrance. She told her maids to drive the jackal away. The jackal rose as if from sleep, and instead of running away, opened his bundle of betel-leaves, put some into his mouth, and began chewing them. The princess and her maids were not a little astonished at the sight. They said among themselves, "What an uncommon jackal is this! From what country can he have come? A jackal chewing betel-leaves! why thousands of men and women of this city cannot indulge in that luxury. He must have come from a wealthy land." The princess asked the jackal, "Sivalu![1] from what country do you come? It must be a very prosperous country where the jackals chew betel-leaves. Do other animals in your country chew betel-leaves?" "Dearest princess," replied the jackal, "I come from a land flowing with milk and honey. Betel-leaves are as plentiful in my country as the grass in your fields. All animals in my country—cows, sheep, dogs—chew betel-leaves. We want no good thing." "Happy is the

[1] A name for a jackal, not unlike Reynard in Europe.

"The jackal . . . opened his bundle of betel-leaves, put some into his mouth, and began chewing them."

WARWICK GOBLE

country," said the princess, "where there is such plenty, and thrice happy the king who rules in it!" "As for our king," said the jackal, "he is the richest king in the world. His palace is like the heaven of Indra. I have seen your palace here; it is a miserable hut compared to the palace of our king." The princess, whose curiosity was excited to the utmost pitch, hastily went through her bath, and going to the apartments of the queen-mother, told her of the wonderful jackal lying at the entrance of the tank. Her curiosity being excited, the jackal was sent for. When the jackal stood in the presence of the queen, he began munching the betel-leaves. "You come," said the queen, "from a very rich country. Is your king married?" "Please your majesty, our king is not married. Princesses from distant parts of the world tried to get married to him, but he rejected them all. Happy will that princess be whom our king condescends to marry!" "Don't you think, Sivalu," asked the queen, "that my daughter is as beautiful as a Peri, and that she is fit to be the wife of the proudest king in the world?" "I quite think," said the jackal, "that the princess is exceedingly handsome; indeed, she is the handsomest princess I have ever seen; but I don't know whether our king will have a liking for her." "Liking for my daughter!" said the queen, "you have only to paint her to him as she is, and he is sure to turn mad with love. To be serious, Sivalu, I am anxious to get my daughter married. Many princes have sought her hand, but I am unwilling to give her to any of them, as they are not the sons of great kings. But your king seems to be a great king. I can have no objection to making him my son-in-law." The queen sent word to the king, requesting him to come and see the jackal. The king came and saw the jackal, heard him describe the wealth and pomp of the king of his country, and expressed himself not unwilling to give away his daughter in marriage to him.

The jackal after this returned to the weaver and said to him, "O lord of the loom, you are the luckiest man in the world; it is all settled; you are to become the son-in-law of a great king. I have told them that you are yourself a great king, and you must behave yourself as one. You must do just as I instruct you, otherwise your fortune will not only not be made, but both you and I will be put to death." "I'll do just as you bid me," said the weaver. The shrewd jackal drew in his own mind a plan of the method of procedure he should adopt, and after a few days went back to the palace of the king in the same manner in which he had gone before, that is to say, chewing betel-leaves and lying down at the entrance of the tank on the premises of the palace. The king and queen were glad to see him, and eagerly asked him as to the success of his mission. The jackal said, "In order to relieve your minds I may tell you at once that my mission has been so far successful. If you only knew the infinite trouble I have had in persuading his Majesty, my sovereign, to make up his mind to marry your daughter, you would give me no end of thanks. For a long time he would not hear of it, but gradually I brought him round. You have now only to fix an auspicious day for the celebration of the solemn rite. There is one bit of advice, however, which I, as your friend, would give you. It is this. My master is so great a king that if he were to come to you in state, attended by all his followers, his horses and his elephants, you would find it impossible to accommodate them all in your palace or in your city. I would therefore propose that our king should come to your city, not in state, but in a private manner; and that you send to the outskirts of your city your own elephants, horses, and conveyances, to bring him and only a few of his followers to your palace." "Many thanks, wise Sivalu, for this advice. I could not possibly make accommodation in my city for the followers of so great a king as your master is. I should be very glad if he did not come in state; and trust you will use your influence to persuade him to come in a private manner; for I should be ruined if he came in state." The jackal then gravely said, "I will do my best in the matter," and then returned to his own village, after the royal astrologer had fixed an auspicious day for the wedding.

On his return the jackal busied himself with making preparations for the great ceremony. As the weaver was clad in tatters, he told him to go to the washermen of the village and borrow from them a suit of clothes. As for himself, he went to the king of his race, and told him that on a certain day he would like one thousand jackals to accompany him to a certain place. He went to the king of crows, and begged that his corvine majesty would be pleased to allow one thousand of his black subjects to accompany him on a certain day to a certain place. He preferred a similar petition to the king of paddy-birds.

At last the great day arrived. The weaver arrayed himself in the clothes which he had borrowed from the village washermen. The jackal made his appearance, accompanied by a train of a thousand jackals, a thousand crows, and a thousand paddy-birds. The nuptial procession started on their journey, and towards sundown arrived within two miles of the king's palace. There the jackal told his friends, the thousand jackals, to set up a loud howl; at his bidding the thousand crows cawed their loudest; while the hoarse screechings of the thousand paddy-birds furnished a suitable accompaniment. The effect may be imagined. They all together made a noise the like of which had never been heard since the world began. While this unearthly noise was going on, the jackal himself hastened to the palace, and asked the king whether he thought he would be able to accommodate the wedding-party, which was about two miles distant, and whose noise was at that moment sounding in his ears. The king said "Impossible, Sivalu; from the sound of the procession I infer there must be at least one hundred thousand souls.

How is it possible to accommodate so many guests? Please, so arrange that the bridegroom only will come to my house." "Very well," said the jackal; "I told you at the beginning that you would not be able to accommodate all the attendants of my august master. I'll do as you wish. My master will alone come in undress. Send a horse for the purpose." The jackal, accompanied by a horse and groom, came to the place where his friend the weaver was, thanked the thousand jackals, the thousand crows, and the thousand paddy-birds, for their valuable services, and told them all to go away, while he himself, and the weaver on horseback, wended their way to the king's palace. The bridal party, waiting in the palace, were greatly disappointed at the personal appearance of the weaver; but the jackal told them that his master had purposely put on a mean dress, as his would-be father-in-law declared himself unable to accommodate the bridegroom and his attendants coming in state. The royal priests now began the interesting ceremony, and the nuptial knot was tied for ever. The bridegroom seldom opened his lips, agreeably to the instructions of the jackal, who was afraid lest his speech should betray him. At night when he was lying in bed he began to count the beams and rafters of the room, and said audibly, "This beam will make a first-rate loom, that other a capital beam, and that yonder an excellent sley." The princess, his bride, was not a little astonished. She began to think in her mind, "Is the man, to whom they have tied me, a king or a weaver?

I am afraid he is the latter ; otherwise why should he be talking of weaver's loom, beam, and sley ? Ah, me ! is this what the fates keep in store for me ? " In the morning the princess related to the queen-mother the weaver's soliloquy. The king and queen, not a little surprised at this recital, took the jackal to task about it. The ready-witted jackal at once said, "Your Majesty need not be surprised at my august master's soliloquy. His palace is surrounded by a population of seven hundred families of the best weavers in the world, to whom he has given rent-free lands, and whose welfare he continually seeks. It must have been in one of his philanthropic moods that he uttered the soliloquy which has taken your Majesty by surprise." The jackal, however, now felt that it was high time for himself and the weaver to decamp with the princess, since the proverbial simplicity of his friend of the loom might any moment involve him in danger. The jackal therefore represented to the king, that weighty affairs of state would not permit his august master to spend another day in the palace ; that he should start for his kingdom that very day with his bride ; and his master was resolved to travel *incognito* on foot, only the princess, now the queen, should leave the city in a *palki.* After a great deal of yea and nay, the king and queen at last consented to the proposal. The party came to the outskirts of the weaver's village ; the *palki* bearers were sent away ; and the princess, who asked where her husband's palace was, was made to walk on foot. The weaver's hut was soon reached, and the jackal, addressing the princess, said, "This, madam, is your husband's palace." The princess began to beat her forehead with the palms of her hands in sheer despair. "Ah, me! is this the husband whom Prajapati[1] intended for me? Death would have been a thousand times better."

As there was nothing for it, the princess soon got reconciled to her fate. She, however, determined to make her husband rich, especially as she knew the secret of becoming rich. One day she told her husband to get for her a pice-worth of flour. She put a little water in the flour, and smeared her body with the paste. When the paste dried on her body, she began wiping the paste with her fingers; and as the paste fell in small balls from her body, it got turned into gold. She repeated this process every day for some time, and thus got an immense quantity of gold. She soon became mistress of more gold than is to be found in the coffers of any king. With this gold she employed a whole army of masons, carpenters and architects, who in no time built one of the finest palaces in the world. Seven hundred families of weavers were sought for and settled round about the palace. After this she wrote a letter to her father to say that she was sorry he had not favoured her with a visit since the day of her marriage, and that she would be delighted if he now came to see her and her husband. The king agreed to come, and a day was fixed. The princess made

[1] The god who presides over marriages.

great preparations against the day of her father's arrival. Hospitals were established in several parts of the town for diseased, sick, and infirm animals. The beasts in thousands were made to chew betel-leaves on the wayside. The streets were covered with Cashmere shawls for her father and his attendants to walk on. There was no end of the display of wealth and grandeur. The king and queen arrived in state, and were infinitely delighted at the apparently boundless riches of their son-in-law. The jackal now appeared on the scene, and saluting the king and queen, said—"Did I not tell you?"

Here my story endeth,
The Natiya-thorn withereth, etc.

XIX

THE BOY WITH THE MOON ON HIS FOREHEAD

THERE was a certain king who had six queens, none of whom bore children. Physicians, holy sages, mendicants, were consulted, countless drugs were had recourse to, but all to no purpose. The king was disconsolate. His ministers told him to marry a seventh wife ; and he was accordingly on the look out.

In the royal city there lived a poor old woman who used to pick up cow-dung from the fields, make it into cakes, dry them in the sun, and sell them in the market for fuel. This was her only means of subsistence. This old woman had a daughter exquisitely beautiful. Her beauty excited the admiration of every one that saw her ; and it was solely in consequence of her surpassing beauty that three young ladies, far above her in rank and station, contracted friendship with her. Those three young ladies were the daughter of the king's minister, the daughter of a wealthy merchant, and the daughter of the royal priest. These three young ladies, together with the daughter of the poor old woman, were one day bathing in a tank not far from the palace. As they were performing their ablutions, each dwelt on her own good qualities. "Look here, sister," said the minister's daughter, addressing the merchant's daughter, "the man that marries me will be a happy man, for he will not have to buy clothes for me. The cloth which I once put on never gets soiled, never gets old, never tears." The merchant's daughter said, "And my husband too will be a happy man, for the fuel which I use in cooking never gets turned into ashes. The same fuel serves from day to day, from year to year." "And my husband will also become a happy man," said the daughter of the royal chaplain, "for the rice which I cook one day never gets finished, and when we have all eaten, the same quantity which was first cooked remains always in the pot." The daughter of the poor old woman said in her turn, "And the man that marries me will also be happy, for I shall give birth to twin children, a son and a daughter. The daughter will be divinely fair, and the son will have the moon on his forehead and stars on the palms of his hands."

The above conversation was overheard by the king, who, as he was on the look out for a seventh queen, used to skulk about in places where women met together. The king thus thought in his mind—"I don't care a straw for the girl whose clothes never tear and never get old; neither do I care for the other girl whose fuel is never consumed ; nor for the third girl whose rice never fails in the pot. But the fourth girl is quite charming ! She will give birth to twin children, a son and a daughter ; the daughter will be divinely fair, and the son will have the moon on his forehead and stars on the palms of his hands. That is the girl I want. I'll make her my wife."

On making inquiries on the same day, the king found that the fourth girl was the daughter of a poor old woman who picked up cow-dung from the fields ; but though there was thus an infinite disparity in rank, he determined to marry her. On the very same day he sent for the poor old woman. She, poor thing, was quite frightened when she saw a messenger of the king standing at the door of her hut. She thought that the king had sent for her to punish her, because, perhaps, she had some day unwittingly picked up the dung of the king's cattle. She went to the palace, and was admitted into the king's private chamber. The king asked her whether she had a very fair daughter, and whether that daughter was the friend of his own minister's and priest's daughters. When the woman answered in the affirmative, he said to her, "I will marry your daughter, and make her my queen." The woman hardly believed her own ears—the thing was so strange. He, however, solemnly declared to her that he had made up his mind, and was determined to marry her daughter. It was soon known in the capital that the king was going to marry the daughter of the old woman who picked up cow-dung in the fields. When the six queens heard the news, they would not believe it, till the king himself told them that the news was true. They thought that the king had somehow got mad. They reasoned with him thus—"What folly, what madness, to marry a girl who is not fit to be our maid-servant! And you expect us to treat her as our equal—a girl whose mother goes about picking up cow-dung in the fields! Surely, my lord, you are beside yourself!" The king's purpose, however, remained unshaken. The royal astrologer was called, and an auspicious day was fixed for the celebration of the king's marriage. On the appointed day the royal priest tied the marital knot, and the daughter of the poor old picker-up of cow-dung in the fields became the seventh and best beloved queen.

Some time after the celebration of the marriage, the king went for six months to another part of his dominions. Before setting out he called to him the seventh queen, and said to her, "I am going away to another part of my dominions for six months. Before the expiration of that period I expect you to be confined. But I should like to be present with you at the time, as your enemies may do mischief. Take this golden bell and hang it in your room. When the pains of childbirth come upon you, ring this bell, and I will be with you in a moment in whatever part of my dominions I may be at the time. Remember, you are to ring the bell only when you feel the pains of childbirth." After saying this the king started on his journey. The six queens, who had overheard the king, went on the next day to the apartments of the seventh queen, and said, "What a nice bell of gold you have got, sister! Where did you get it, and why have you hung it up?" The seventh queen, in her simplicity, said, "The king has given it to me, and if I were to ring it, the king would immediately come to me wherever he might be at the time." "Impossible!" said the six queens, "you must have misunderstood the king. Who can believe that this bell can be heard at the distance of hundreds of miles? Besides, if it could be heard, how would the king be able to travel a great distance in the twinkling of an eye? This must be a hoax. If you ring the bell, you will find that what the king said was pure nonsense." The six queens then told her to make a trial. At first she was unwilling, remembering what the king had told her; but at last she was prevailed upon to ring the bell. The king was at the moment half-way to the capital of his other dominions, but at the ringing of the bell he stopped short in his journey, turned back, and in no time stood in the queen's apartments. Finding the queen going about in her rooms, he asked why she had rung the bell though her hour had not come. She, without informing the king of the entreaty of the six queens, replied that she rang the bell only to see whether what he had said was true. The king was somewhat indignant, told her distinctly not to ring the bell again till the moment of the coming upon her of the pains of childbirth, and then went away. After the lapse of some weeks the six queens again begged of the seventh queen to make a second trial of the bell. They said to her, "The first time when you rang the bell, the king was only at a short distance from you, it was therefore easy for him to hear the bell and to come to you; but now he has long ago settled in his other capital, let us see if he will now hear the bell and come to you." She resisted for a long time, but was at last prevailed upon by them to ring the bell. When the sound of the bell reached the king he was in court dispensing justice, but when he heard the sound of the bell (and no one else heard it) he closed the court and in no time stood in the queen's apartments. Finding that the queen was not about to be confined, he asked her why she had again rung the bell before her hour. She, without saying anything of the importunities of the six queens, replied that she merely made a second trial of the bell. The king became very angry, and said to her, "Now listen, since you have called me twice for nothing, let it be known to you that when the throes of childbirth do really come upon you, and you ring the bell ever so lustily, I will not come to you. You must be left to your fate." The king then went away.

At last the day of the seventh queen's deliverance arrived. On first feeling the pains she rang the golden bell. She waited, but the king did not make his appearance. She rang again with all her might, still the king did not make his appearance. The king certainly did hear the sound of the bell; but he did not come as he was displeased with the queen. When the six queens saw that the king did not come, they went to the seventh queen and told her that it was not customary with the ladies of the palace to be confined in the king's apartments; she must go to a hut near the stables. They then sent for the midwife of the palace, and heavily bribed her to make away with the infant the moment it should be born into the world. The seventh queen gave birth to a son who had the moon on his forehead and stars on the palms of his hands, and also to an uncommonly beautiful girl. The midwife had come provided with a couple of newly born pups. She put the pups before the mother, saying—"You have given birth to these," and took away the twin-children in an earthen vessel. The queen was quite insensible at the time, and did not notice the twins at the time they were carried away. The king, though he was angry with the seventh queen, yet remembering that she was destined to give birth to the heir of his throne, changed his mind, and came to see her the next morning. The pups were produced before the king as the offspring of the queen. The king's anger and vexation knew no bounds. He ordered that the seventh queen should be expelled from the palace, that she should be clothed in leather, and that she should be employed in the market-place to drive away crows and to keep off dogs. Though scarcely able to move she was driven away from the palace, stripped of her fine robes, clothed in leather, and set to drive away the crows of the market-place.

The midwife, when she put the twins in the earthen vessel, bethought herself of the best way to destroy them. She did not think it proper to throw them into a tank, lest they should be discovered the next day. Neither did she think of burying them in the ground, lest they should be dug up by a jackal and exposed to the gaze of people. The best way to make an end of them, she thought, would be to burn them, and reduce them to ashes, that no trace might be left of them. But how could she, at that dead hour of night, burn them without some other person helping her? A happy thought struck her. There was a potter on the outskirts of the city, who used during the day to mould vessels of clay on his wheel, and burn them during the latter part of the night. The midwife thought that the best plan would be to put the vessel with the twins along with the unburnt clay vessels which the potter had arranged in order and gone to sleep expecting to get up late at night and set them on fire; in this way, she thought, the twins would be reduced to ashes. She, accordingly, put the vessel with the twins along with the unburnt clay vessels of the potter, and went away.

Somehow or other, that night the potter and his wife overslept themselves. It was near the break of day when the potter's wife, awaking out of sleep, roused her husband, and said, "Oh, my good man, we have overslept ourselves; it is now near morning and I much fear it is now too late to set the pots on fire." Hastily unbolting the door of her cottage, she rushed out to the place where the pots were ranged in rows. She could scarcely believe her eyes when she saw that all the pots had been baked and were looking bright red, though neither she nor her husband had applied any fire to them. Wondering at her good luck, and not knowing what to make of it, she ran to her husband and said, "Just come and see!" The potter came, saw, and wondered. The pots had never before been so well baked. Who could have done this? This could have proceeded only from some god or goddess. Fumbling about the pots, he accidentally upturned one in which, lo and behold, were seen huddled up together two newly born infants of unearthly beauty. The potter said to his wife, "My dear, you must pretend to have given birth to these beautiful children." Accordingly all arrangements were made, and in due time it was given out that the twins had been born to her. And such lovely twins they were! On the same day many women of the neighbourhood came to see the potter's wife and the twins to which she had given birth, and to offer their congratulations on this unexpected good fortune. As for the potter's wife, she could not be too proud of her pretended children, and said to her admiring friends, "I had hardly hoped to have children at all. But now that the gods have given me these twins, may they receive the blessings of you all, and live for ever!"

The twins grew and were strengthened. The brother and sister, when they played about in the fields and lanes, were the admiration of every one who saw them; and all wondered at the uncommonly good luck of the potter in being blessed with such angelic children. They were about twelve years old when the potter, their reputed father, became dangerously ill. It was evident to all that his sickness would end in death. The potter, perceiving his last end approaching, said to his wife, "My dear, I am going the way of all the earth; but I am leaving to you enough to live upon; live on and take care of these children." The woman said to her husband, "I am not going to survive you. Like all good and faithful wives, I am determined to die along with you. You and I will burn together on the same funeral pyre. As for the children, they are old enough to take care of themselves, and you are leaving them enough money." Her friends tried to dissuade her from her purpose, but in vain. The potter died; and as his remains were being burnt, his wife, now a widow, threw herself on the pyre, and burnt herself to death.

The boy with the moon on his forehead—by the way, he always kept his head covered with a turban lest the halo should attract notice—and his sister, now broke up the potter's establishment, sold the wheel and the pots and pans, and went to the bazaar in the king's city. The moment they entered, the bazaar was lit up on a sudden. The shopkeepers of the bazaar were greatly surprised.

WARWICK

"A bright light, like that of the moon, was seen shining on his forehead."

They thought some divine beings must have entered the place. They looked upon the beautiful boy and his sister with wonder. They begged of them to stay in the bazaar. They built a house for them. When they used to ramble about, they were always followed at a distance by the woman clothed in leather, who was appointed by the king to drive away the crows of the bazaar. By some unaccountable impulse she used also to hang about the house in which they lived. The boy in a short time bought a horse, and went a-hunting in the neighbouring forests. One day while he was hunting, the king was also hunting in the same forest, and seeing a brother huntsman the king drew near to him. The king was struck with the beauty of the lad and a yearning for him the moment he saw him. As a deer went past, the youth shot an arrow, and the reaction of the force necessary to shoot the arrow made the turban of his head fall off, on which a bright light, like that of the moon, was seen shining on his forehead. The king saw, and immediately thought of the son with the moon on his forehead and stars on the palms of his hands who was to have been born of his seventh queen. The youth on letting fly the arrow galloped off, in spite of the earnest entreaty of the king to wait and speak to him. The king went home a sadder man than he came out of it. He became very moody and melancholy. The six queens asked him why he was looking so sad. He told them that he had seen in the woods a lad with the moon on his forehead, which reminded him of the son who was to be born of the seventh queen. The six queens tried to comfort him in the best way they could; but they wondered who the youth could be. Was it possible that the twins were living? Did not the midwife say that she had burnt both the son and the daughter to ashes? Who, then, could this lad be? The midwife was sent for by the six queens and questioned. She swore that she had seen the twins burnt. As for the lad whom the king had met with, she would soon find out who he was. On making inquiries, the midwife soon found out that two strangers were living in the bazaar in a house which the shopkeepers had built for them. She entered the house and saw the girl only, as the lad had again gone out a-shooting. She pretended to be their aunt, who had gone away to another part of the country shortly after their birth; she had been searching after them for a long time, and was now glad to find them in the king's city near the palace. She greatly admired the beauty of the girl, and said to her, "My dear child, you are so beautiful, you require the *kataki*[1] flower properly to set off your beauty. You should tell your brother to plant a row of that flower in this court-yard." "What flower is that, auntie? I never saw it." "How could you have seen it, my child? It is not found here; it grows on the other side of the ocean, guarded by seven hundred Rakshasas." "How, then," said the girl, "will

[1] *Calotropis gigantea.*

"The six queens tried to comfort him."

WARWICK GOBLE

my brother get it?" "He may try to get it, if you speak to him," replied the woman. The woman made this proposal in the hope that the boy with the moon on his forehead would perish in the attempt to get the flower.

When the youth with the moon on his forehead returned from hunting, his sister told him of the visit paid to her by their aunt, and requested him, if possible, to get for her the *kataki* flower. He was sceptical about the existence of any aunt of theirs in the world, but he was resolved that, to please his beloved sister, he would get the flower on which she had set her heart. Next morning, accordingly, he started on his journey, after bidding his sister not to stir out of the house till his return. He rode on his fleet steed, which was of the *pakshiraj*[1] tribe, and soon reached the outskirts of what seemed to him dense forests of interminable length. He descried some Rakshasas prowling about. He went to some distance, shot with his arrows some deer and rhinoceroses in the neighbouring thickets, and, approaching the place where the Rakshasas were prowling about, called out, "O auntie dear, O auntie dear, your nephew is here." A huge Rakshasi came towards him and said, "O, you are the youth with the moon on your forehead and stars on the palms of your hands. We were all expecting you, but as you have called me aunt, I will not eat you up. What is it you want? Have you brought any eatables

[1] Literally the *king of birds*, a fabulous species of horse remarkable for their swiftness.

for me?" The youth gave her the deer and rhinoceroses which he had killed. Her mouth watered at the sight of the dead animals, and she began eating them. After swallowing down all the carcases, she said, "Well, what do you want?" The youth said, "I want some *kataki* flowers for my sister." She then told him that it would be difficult for him to get the flower, as it was guarded by seven hundred Rakshasas; however, he might make the attempt, but in the first instance he must go to his uncle on the north side of that forest. While the youth was going to his uncle of the north, on the way he killed some deer and rhinoceroses, and seeing a gigantic Rakshasa at some distance, cried out, "Uncle dear, uncle dear, your nephew is here. Auntie has sent me to you." The Rakshasa came near and said, "You are the youth with the moon on your forehead and stars on the palms of your hands; I would have swallowed you outright, had you not called me uncle, and had you not said that your aunt had sent you to me. Now, what is it you want?" The savoury deer and rhinoceroses were then presented to him; he ate them all, and then listened to the petition of the youth. The youth wanted the *kataki* flower. The Rakshasa said, "You want the *kataki* flower! Very well, try and get it if you can. After passing through this forest, you will come to an impenetrable forest of *kachiri*.[1] You will say to that forest, 'O mother *kachiri!* please make way for me, or else I die.'

[1] *Arum fornicatum.*

On that the forest will open up a passage for you. You will next come to the ocean. You will say to the ocean, 'O mother ocean ! please make way for me, or else I die,' and the ocean will make way for you. After crossing the ocean, you enter the gardens where the *kataki* blooms. Good-bye ; do as I have told you." The youth thanked his Rakshasa-uncle, and went on his way. After he had passed through the forest, he saw before him an impenetrable forest of *kachiri*. It was so close and thick, and withal so bristling with thorns, that not a mouse could go through it. Remembering the advice of his uncle, he stood before the forest with folded hands, and said, "O mother *kachiri !* please make way for me, or else I die." On a sudden a clean path was opened up in the forest, and the youth gladly passed through it. The ocean now lay before him. He said to the ocean, "O mother ocean ! make way for me, or else I die." Forthwith the waters of the ocean stood up on two sides like two walls, leaving an open passage between them, and the youth passed through dryshod.

Now, right before him were the gardens of the *kataki* flower. He entered the inclosure, and found himself in a spacious palace which seemed to be unoccupied. On going from apartment to apartment he found a young lady of more than earthly beauty sleeping on a bedstead of gold. He went near, and noticed two little sticks, one of gold and the other of silver, lying in the bedstead. The silver stick lay near the feet of the sleeping beauty, and the golden one near the head. He took up the sticks in his hands, and as he was examining them, the golden stick accidentally fell upon the feet of the lady. In a moment the lady woke and sat up, and said to the youth, "Stranger, how have you come to this dismal place? I know who you are, and I know your history. You are the youth with the moon on your forehead and stars on the palms of your hands. Flee, flee from this place! This is the residence of seven hundred Rakshasas who guard the gardens of the *kataki* flower. They have all gone a-hunting; they will return by sundown; and if they find you here you will be eaten up. One Rakshasi brought me from the earth where my father is king. She loves me very dearly, and will not let me go away. By means of these gold and silver sticks she kills me when she goes away in the morning, and by means of those sticks she revives me when she returns in the evening. Flee, flee hence, or you die!" The youth told the young lady how his sister wished very much to have the *kataki* flower, how he passed through the forest of *kachiri*, and how he crossed the ocean. He said also that he was determined not to go alone, he must take the young lady along with him. The remaining part of the day they spent together in rambling about the gardens. As the time was drawing near when the Rakshasas should return, the youth buried himself amid an enormous heap of *kataki* flower which lay in an adjoining apartment, after killing the young lady by touching her head with the golden stick. Just after sunset the youth heard the sound as of a mighty tempest : it was the return of the seven hundred Rakshasas into the gardens. One of them entered the apartment of the young lady, revived her, and said, "I smell a human being, I smell a human being." The young lady replied, "How can a human being come to this place ? I am the only human being here." The Rakshasi then stretched herself on the floor, and told the young lady to shampoo her legs. As she was going on shampooing, she let fall a tear-drop on the Rakshasi's leg. "Why are you weeping, my dear child ?" asked the raw-eater ; "why are you weeping ? Is anything troubling you ?" "No, mamma," answered the young lady, "nothing is troubling me. What can trouble me, when you have made me so comfortable ? I was only thinking what will become of me when you die." "When I die, child ?" said the Rakshasi ; "shall I die ? Yes, of course all creatures die ; but the death of a Rakshasa or Rakshasi will never happen. You know, child, that deep tank in the middle part of these gardens. Well, at the bottom of that tank there is a wooden box, in which there are a male and a female bee. It is ordained by fate that if a human being who has the moon on his forehead and stars on the palms of his hands were to come here and dive into that tank, and get hold of the same wooden box, and crush to death the male and female bees without letting a drop of their blood fall to the ground, then we should die. But the accomplishment of this decree of fate is, I think, impossible. For, in the first place, there can be no such human being who will have the moon on his forehead and stars on the palms of his hands; and, in the second place, if there be such a man, he will find it impossible to come to this place, guarded as it is by seven hundred of us, encompassed by a deep ocean, and barricaded by an impervious forest of *kachiri*—not to speak of the outposts and sentinels that are stationed on the other side of the forest. And then, even if he succeeds in coming here, he will perhaps not know the secret of the wooden box; and even if he knows of the secret of the wooden box, he may not succeed in killing the bees without letting a drop of their blood fall on the ground. And woe be to him if a drop does fall on the ground, for in that case he will be torn up into seven hundred pieces by us. You see then, child, that we are almost immortal—not actually, but virtually so. You may, therefore, dismiss your fears."

On the next morning the Rakshasi got up, killed the young lady by means of the sticks, and went away in search of food along with other Rakshasas and Rakshasis. The lad, who had the moon on his forehead and stars on the palms of his hands, came out of the heap of flowers and revived the young lady. The young lady recited to the young man the whole of the conversation she had had with the Rakshasi. It was a perfect revelation to him. He, however, lost no time in beginning to act. He shut the heavy gates of the gardens. He dived into the tank and brought up the wooden box. He opened the wooden box, and caught hold of the male and female bees as they were about to escape. He crushed them on the palms of his hands, besmearing his body with every drop of their blood. The moment this was done, loud cries and groans were heard around about the inclosure of the gardens. Agreeably to the decree of fate all the Rakshasas approached the gardens and fell down dead. The youth with the moon on his forehead took as many *kataki* flowers as he could, together with their seeds, and left the palace, around which were lying in mountain heaps the carcases of the mighty dead, in company with the young and beautiful lady. The waters of the ocean retreated before the youth as before, and the forest of *kachiri* also opened up a passage through it ; and the happy couple reached the house in the bazaar, where they were welcomed by the sister of the youth who had the moon on his forehead.

On the following morning the youth, as usual, went to hunt. The king was also there. A deer passed by, and the youth shot an arrow. As he shot, the turban as usual fell off his head, and a bright light issued from it. The king saw and wondered. He told the youth to stop, as he wished to contract friendship with him. The youth told him to come to his house, and gave him his address. The king went to the house of the youth in the middle of the day. Pushpavati —for that was the name of the young lady that had been brought from beyond the ocean—told the king—for she knew the whole history—how his seventh queen had been persuaded by the other six queens to ring the bell twice before her time, how she was delivered of a beautiful boy and girl, how pups were substituted in their room, how the twins were saved in a miraculous manner in the house of the potter, how they were well treated in the bazaar, and how the youth with the moon on his forehead rescued her from the clutches of the Rakshasas. The king, mightily incensed with the six queens, had them, on the following day, buried alive in the ground. The seventh queen was then brought from the market-place and reinstated in her position ; and the youth with the moon on his forehead, and the lovely Pushpavati and their sister, lived happily together.

Here my story endeth,
The Natiya-thorn withereth, etc.

XX

THE GHOST WHO WAS AFRAID OF BEING BAGGED

ONCE on a time there lived a barber who had a wife. They did not live happily together, as the wife always complained that she had not enough to eat. Many were the curtain lectures which were inflicted upon the poor barber. The wife used often to say to her mate, "If you had not the means to support a wife, why did you marry me? People who have not means ought not to indulge in the luxury of a wife. When I was in my father's house I had plenty to eat, but it seems that I have come to your house to fast. Widows only fast; I have become a widow in your life-time." She was not content with mere words; she got very angry one day and struck her husband with the broomstick of the house. Stung with shame, and abhorring himself on account of his wife's reproach and beating, he left his house, with the implements of his craft, and vowed never to return and see his wife's face again till he had become rich. He went from village to village, and towards nightfall came to the outskirts of a forest. He laid himself down at the foot of a tree, and spent many a sad hour in bemoaning his hard lot.

It so chanced that the tree, at the foot of which the barber was lying down, was dwelt in by a ghost. The ghost seeing a human being at the foot of the tree naturally thought of destroying him. With this intention the ghost alighted from the tree, and, with outspread arms and a gaping mouth, stood like a tall palmyra tree before the barber, and said, "Now, barber, I am going to destroy you. Who will protect you?" The barber, though quaking in every limb through fear, and his hair standing erect, did not lose his presence of mind, but, with that promptitude and shrewdness which are characteristic of his fraternity, replied, "O spirit, you will destroy me! wait a bit and I'll show you how many ghosts I have captured this very night and put into my bag; and right glad am I to find you here, as I shall have one more ghost in my bag." So saying the barber produced from his bag a small looking-glass, which he always carried about with him along with his razors, his whet-stone, his strop and other utensils, to enable his customers to see whether their beards had been well shaved or not. He stood up, placed the looking-glass right against the face of the ghost, and said, "Here you see one ghost which I have seized and bagged; I am going to put you also in the bag to keep this ghost company." The ghost, seeing his own face in the

" 'Now, barber, I am going to destroy you.
Who will protect you?' "

WARWICK GOBLE

looking-glass, was convinced of the truth of what the barber had said, and was filled with fear. He said to the barber, "O, sir barber, I'll do whatever you bid me, only do not put me into your bag. I'll give you whatever you want." The barber said, "You ghosts are a faithless set, there is no trusting you. You will promise, and not give what you promise." "O, sir," replied the ghost, "be merciful to me; I'll bring to you whatever you order; and if I do not bring it, then put me into your bag." "Very well," said the barber, "bring me just now one thousand gold mohurs; and by to-morrow night you must raise a granary in my house, and fill it with paddy. Go and get the gold mohurs immediately: and if you fail to do my bidding you will certainly be put into my bag." The ghost gladly consented to the conditions. He went away, and in the course of a short time returned with a bag containing a thousand gold mohurs. The barber was delighted beyond measure at the sight of the gold mohurs. He then told the ghost to see to it that by the following night a granary was erected in his house and filled with paddy.

It was during the small hours of the morning that the barber, loaded with the heavy treasure, knocked at the door of his house. His wife, who reproached herself for having in a fit of rage struck her husband with a broomstick, got out of bed and unbolted the door. Her surprise was great when she saw her husband pour out of the bag a glittering heap of gold mohurs.

The next night the poor devil, through fear of being bagged, raised a large granary in the barber's house, and spent the live-long night in carrying on his back large packages of paddy till the granary was filled up to the brim. The uncle of this terrified ghost, seeing his worthy nephew carrying on his back loads of paddy, asked what the matter was. The ghost related what had happened. The uncle-ghost then said, "You fool, you think the barber can bag you! The barber is a cunning fellow; he has cheated you, like a simpleton as you are." "You doubt," said the nephew-ghost, "the power of the barber! come and see." The uncle-ghost then went to the barber's house, and peeped into it through a window. The barber, perceiving from the blast of wind which the arrival of the ghost had produced that a ghost was at the window, placed full before it the self-same looking-glass, saying, "Come now, I'll put you also into the bag." The uncle-ghost, seeing his own face in the looking-glass, got quite frightened, and promised that very night to raise another granary and to fill it, not this time with paddy, but with rice. So in two nights the barber became a rich man, and lived happily with his wife begetting sons and daughters.

Here my story endeth,
The Natiya-thorn withereth, etc.

XXI

THE FIELD OF BONES

ONCE on a time there lived a king who had a son. The young prince had three friends, the son of the prime minister, the son of the prefect of the police, and the son of the richest merchant of the city. These four friends had great love for one another. Once on a time they bethought themselves of seeing distant lands. They accordingly set out one day, each one riding on a horse. They rode on and on, till about noon they came to the outskirts of what seemed to be a dense forest. There they rested a while, tying to the trees their horses, which began to browse. When they had refreshed themselves, they again mounted their horses and resumed their journey. At sunset they saw in the depths of the forest a temple, near which they dismounted, wishing to lodge there that night. Inside the temple there was a *sannyasi*,[1] apparently absorbed in meditation, as he did not notice the four friends. When darkness covered the forest, a light was seen inside the temple. The four friends

[1] Religious devotee.

resolved to pass the night on the balcony of the temple; and as the forest was infested with many wild beasts, they deemed it safe that each of them should watch one *prahara*[1] of the night, while the rest should sleep. It fell to the lot of the merchant's son to watch during the first *prahara*, that is to say, from six in the evening to nine o'clock at night. Towards the end of his watch the merchant's son saw a wonderful sight. The hermit took up a bone with his hand, and repeated over it some words which the merchant's son distinctly heard. The moment the words were uttered, a clattering sound was heard in the precincts of the temple, and the merchant's son saw many bones moving from different parts of the forest. The bones collected themselves inside the temple, at the foot of the hermit, and lay there in a heap. As soon as this took place, the watch of the merchant's son came to an end; and, rousing the son of the prefect of the police, he laid himself down to sleep.

The prefect's son, when he began his watch, saw the hermit sitting cross-legged, wrapped in meditation, near a heap of bones, the history of which he, of course, did not know. For a long time nothing happened. The dead stillness of the night was broken only by the howl of the hyæna and the wolf, and the growl of the tiger. When his time was nearly up he saw a wonderful sight. The hermit looked at the heap of bones lying before him, and uttered some words which the

[1] Eighth part of twenty-four hours, that is, three hours.

prefect's son distinctly heard. No sooner had the words been uttered than a noise was heard among the bones, "and behold a shaking, and the bones came together, bone to its bone"; and the bones which were erewhile lying together in a heap now took the form of a skeleton. Struck with wonder, the prefect's son would have watched longer, but his time was over. He therefore laid himself down to sleep, after rousing the minister's son, to whom, however, he told nothing of what he had seen, as the merchant's son had not told him anything of what he had seen.

The minister's son got up, rubbed his eyes, and began watching. It was the dead hour of midnight, when ghosts, hobgoblins, and spirits of every name and description, go roaming over the wide world, and when all creation, both animate and inanimate, is in deep repose. Even the howl of the wolf and the hyæna and the growl of the tiger had ceased. The minister's son looked towards the temple, and saw the hermit sitting wrapt up in meditation; and near him lying something which seemed to be the skeleton of some animal. He looked towards the dense forest and the darkness all around, and his hair stood on end through terror. In this state of fear and trembling he spent nearly three hours, when an uncommon sight in the temple attracted his notice. The hermit, looking at the skeleton before him, uttered some words which the minister's son distinctly heard. As soon as the words were uttered, "lo, the sinews and the flesh came up upon the bones, and the skin covered them above" ; but there was no breath in the skeleton. Astonished at the sight, the minister's son would have sat up longer, but his time was up. He therefore laid himself down to sleep, after having roused the king's son, to whom, however, he said nothing of what he had seen and heard.

The king's son, when he began his watch, saw the hermit sitting, completely absorbed in devotion, near a figure which looked like some animal, but he was not a little surprised to see the animal lying apparently lifeless, without showing any of the symptoms of life. The prince spent his hours agreeably enough, especially as he had had a long sleep, and as he felt none of that depression which the dead hour of midnight sheds on the spirits ; and he amused himself with marking how the shades of darkness were becoming thinner and paler every moment. But just as he noticed a red streak in the east, he heard a sound from inside the temple. He turned his eyes towards the hermit. The hermit, looking towards the inanimate figure of the animal lying before him, uttered some words which the prince distinctly heard. The moment the words were spoken, "breath came into the animal ; it lived, it stood up upon its feet" ; and quickly rushed out of the temple into the forest. That moment the crows cawed ; the watch of the prince came to an end ; his three companions were roused ; and after a short time they mounted their horses, and resumed their journey, each one thinking of the strange sight seen in the temple.

They rode on and on through the dense and interminable forest, and hardly spoke to one another, till about mid-day they halted under a tree near a pool for refreshment. After they had refreshed themselves with eating some fruits of the forest and drinking water from the pool, the prince said to his three companions, "Friends, did you not see something in the temple of the devotee? I'll tell you what I saw, but first let me hear what you all saw. Let the merchant's son first tell us what he saw as he had the first watch; and the others will follow in order."

Merchant's son. I'll tell you what I saw. I saw the hermit take up a bone in his hand, and repeat some words which I well remember. The moment those words were uttered, a clattering sound was heard in the precincts of the temple, and I saw many bones running into the temple from different directions. The bones collected themselves together inside the temple at the feet of the hermit, and lay there in a heap. I would have gladly remained longer to see the end, but my time was up, and I had to rouse my friend, the son of the prefect of the police.

Prefect's son. Friends, this is what I saw. The hermit looked at the heap of bones lying before him, and uttered some words which I well remember. No sooner had the words been uttered than I heard a noise among the bones, and, strange to say, the bones jumped up, each bone joined itself to its fellow, and the heap became a perfect skeleton. At that moment my watch came to an end, and I had to rouse my respected friend the minister's son.

Minister's son. Well, when I began my watch I saw the said skeleton lying near the hermit. After three mortal hours, during which I was in great fear, I saw the hermit lift his eyes towards the skeleton and utter some words which I well remember. As soon as the words were uttered the skeleton was covered with flesh and hair, but it did not show any symptom of life, as it lay motionless. Just then my watch ended, and I had to rouse my royal friend the prince.

King's son. Friends, from what you yourselves saw, you can guess what I saw. I saw the hermit turn towards the skeleton covered with skin and hair, and repeat some words which I well remember. The moment the words were uttered, the skeleton stood up on its feet, and it looked a fine and lusty deer, and while I was admiring its beauty, it skipped out of the temple, and ran into the forest. That moment the crows cawed.

The four friends, after hearing one another's story, congratulated themselves on the possession of supernatural power, and they did not doubt but that if they pronounced the words which they had heard the hermit utter, the utterance would be followed by the same results. But they resolved to verify their power by an actual experiment. Near the foot of the tree they found a bone lying on the ground, and they accordingly resolved to experiment upon it. The merchant's son took up the bone, and repeated over it the formula he had heard from the hermit. Wonderful to relate, a hundred bones immediately came rushing from different directions, and lay in a heap at the foot of the tree. The son of the prefect of the police then looking upon the heap of bones, repeated the formula which he had heard from the hermit, and forthwith there was a shaking among the bones; the several bones joined themselves together, and formed themselves into a skeleton, and it was the skeleton of a quadruped. The minister's son then drew near the skeleton, and, looking intently upon it, pronounced over it the formula which he had heard from the hermit. The skeleton immediately was covered with flesh, skin, and hair, and, horrible to relate, the animal proved itself to be a royal tiger of the largest size. The four friends were filled with consternation. If the king's son were, by the repetition of the formula he had heard from the hermit, to make the beast alive, it might prove fatal to them all. The three friends, therefore, tried to dissuade the prince from giving life to the tiger. But the prince would not comply with the request. He naturally said, "The *mantras*[1] which you have learned have been proved true and efficacious. But how shall I know that the *mantra* which I have learned is equally efficacious? I must have my *mantra* verified. Nor is it certain that we shall lose our lives by the experiment. Here is this high tree. You can climb into its topmost branches, and I shall also follow you thither after pronouncing the *mantra*." In vain

[1] Charm or incantation.

did the three friends dwell upon the extreme danger attending the experiment: the prince remained inexorable. The minister's son, the prefect's son, and the merchant's son climbed up into the topmost branches of the tree, while the king's son went up to the middle of the tree. From there, looking intently upon the lifeless tiger, he pronounced the words which he had learned from the hermit, and quickly ran up the tree. In the twinkling of an eye the tiger stood upright, gave out a terrible growl, with a tremendous spring killed all the four horses which were browsing at a little distance, and, dragging one of them, rushed towards the densest part of the forest. The four friends ensconced on the branches of the tree were almost petrified with fear at the sight of the terrible tiger; but the danger was now over. The tiger went off at a great distance from them, and from its growl they judged that it must be at least two miles distance from them. After a little they came down from the tree; and as they now had no horses on which to ride, they walked on foot through the forest, till, coming to its end, they reached the shore of the sea. They sat on the sea-shore hoping to see some ship sailing by. They had not sat long, when fortunately they descried a vessel in the offing. They waved their handkerchiefs, and made all sorts of signs to attract the notice of the people on board the ship. The captain and the crew noticed the men on the shore. They came towards the shore, took the men upon board, but added that as they were short of

WARWICK GOBLE

"They approached a magnificent pile of buildings."

provisions they could not have them a long time on board, but would put them ashore at the first port they came to. After four or five days' voyage, they saw not far from the shore high buildings and turrets, and supposing the place to be a large city, the four friends landed there.

The four friends, immediately after landing, walked along a long avenue of stately trees, at the end of which was a bazaar. There were hundreds of shops in the bazaar, but not a single human being in them. There were sweetmeat shops in which there were heaps of confectioneries ranged in regular rows, but no human beings to sell them. There was the blacksmith's shop, there was the anvil, there were the bellows and the other tools of the smithy, but there was no smith there. There were stalls in which there were heaps of faded and dried vegetables, but no men or women to sell them. The streets were all deserted, no human beings, no cattle were to be seen there. There were carts, but no bullocks; there were carriages, but no horses. The doors and windows of the houses of the city on both sides of the streets were all open, but no human being was visible in them. It seemed to be a deserted city. It seemed to be a city of the dead—and all the dead taken out and buried. The four friends were astonished—they were frightened at the sight. As they went on, they approached a magnificent pile of buildings, which seemed to be the palace of a king. They went to the gate and to the porter's lodge. They saw shields, swords, spears, and other weapons suspended in the lodge, but no porters. They entered the premises, but saw no guards, no human beings. They went to the stables, saw the troughs, grain, and grass lying about in profusion, but no horses. They went inside the palace, passed the long corridors—still no human being was visible. They went through six long courts—still no human being. They entered the seventh court, and there and then, for the first time, did they see living human beings. They saw coming towards them four princesses of matchless beauty. Each of these four princesses caught hold of the arm of each of the four friends; and each princess called each man whom she had caught hold of her husband. The princesses said that they had been long waiting for the four friends, and expressed great joy at their arrival. The princesses took the four friends into the innermost apartments, and gave them a sumptuous feast. There were no servants attending them, the princesses themselves bringing in the provisions and setting them before the four friends. At the outset the four princesses told the four friends that no questions were to be asked about the depopulation of the city. After this, each princess went into her private apartment along with her newly-found husband. Shortly after the prince and princess had retired into their private apartment, the princess began to shed tears. On the prince inquiring into the cause, the princess said, "O prince! I pity you very much. You seem, by your bearing, to be the son of a king, and you have, no doubt, the heart of a king's son ; I will therefore tell you my whole story, and the story of my three companions who look like princesses. I am the daughter of a king, whose palace this is, and those three creatures, who are dressed like princesses, and who have called your three friends their husbands, are Rakshasis. They came to this city some time ago ; they ate up my father, the king, my mother, the queen, my brothers, my sisters, of whom I had a large number. They ate up the king's ministers and servants. They ate up gradually all the people of the city, all my father's horses and elephants, and all the cattle of the city. You must have noticed, as you came to the palace, that there are no human beings, no cattle, no living thing in this city. They have all been eaten up by those three Rakshasis. They have spared me alone—and that, I suppose, only for a time. When the Rakshasis saw you and your friends from a distance, they were very glad, as they mean to eat you all up after a short time."

King's son. But if this is the case, how do I know that you are not a Rakshasi yourself? Perhaps you mean to swallow me up by throwing me off my guard.

Princess. I'll mention one fact which proves that those three creatures are Rakshasis, while I am not. Rakshasis, you know, eat food a hundred times larger in quantity than men or women. What the Rakshasis eat at table along with us is not sufficient to appease their hunger. They therefore go out at night to distant lands in search of men or cattle, as there are none in this city. If you ask your friends to watch and see whether their wives remain all night in their beds, they will find they go out and stay away a good part of the night, whereas you will find me the whole night with you. But please see that the Rakshasis do not get the slightest inkling of all this; for if they hear of it, they will kill me in the first instance, and afterwards swallow you all up.

The next day the king's son called together the minister's son, the prefect's son, and the merchant's son, and held a consultation, enjoining the strictest secrecy on all. He told them what he had heard from the princess, and requested them to lie awake in their beds to watch whether their pretended princesses went out at night or not. One presumptive argument in favour of the assertion of the princess was that all the pretended princesses were fast asleep during the whole of the day in consequence of their nightly wanderings, whereas the female friend of the king's son did not sleep at all during the day. The three friends accordingly lay in their beds at night pretending to be asleep and manifesting all the symptoms of deep sleep. Each one observed that his female friend at a certain hour, thinking her mate to be in deep sleep, left the room, stayed away the whole night, and returned to her bed only at dawn. During the following day each female friend slept out nearly the whole day, and woke up only in the afternoon. For two nights and days the three friends observed this. The king's son also remained awake at night pretending to be asleep, but the princess was not observed for a single moment to leave the room, nor was she observed to sleep in the day. From these circumstances the friends of the king's son began to suspect that their partners were really Rakshasis as the princess said they were.

By way of confirmation the princess also told the king's son, that the Rakshasis, after eating the flesh of men and animals, threw the bones towards the north of the city, where there was an immense collection of them. The king's son and his three friends went one day towards that part of the city, and sure enough they saw there immense heaps of the bones of men and animals piled up into hills. From this they became more and more convinced that the three women were Rakshasis in deed and truth.

The question now was how to run away from these devourers of men and animals? There was one circumstance greatly in favour of the four friends, and that was, that the three Rakshasis slept during nearly the whole day; they had therefore the greater part of the day for the maturing of their plans. The princess advised them to go towards the sea-shore, and watch if any ships sailed that way. The four friends accordingly used to go to the sea-shore looking for ships. They were always accompanied by the princess, who took the precaution of carrying with her in a bundle her most valuable jewels, pearls and precious stones. It happened one day that they saw a ship passing at a great distance from the shore. They made signs which attracted the notice of the captain and crew. The ship came towards the land, and the four friends and princess were, after much entreaty, taken up. The princess exhorted the crew to row with all their might, for which she promised them a handsome reward; for she knew that the Rakshasis would awake in the afternoon, and immediately come after the ship; and they would assuredly catch hold of the vessel and destroy all the crew and passengers if it stood short of eighty miles from land, for the Rakshasis had the power of distending their bodies to the length of ten *Yojanas*.[1] The four friends and the princess cheered on the crew, and the oarsmen rowed with all their might; and the ship, favoured by the wind, shot over the deep like lightning. It was near sun-down when a terrible yell was heard on the shore. The Rakshasis had wakened from their sleep, and not finding either the four friends or the princess, naturally thought they had got hold of a ship and were escaping. They therefore ran along the shore with lightning rapidity, and seeing the ship afar off they distended their bodies. But fortunately the vessel was more than eighty miles off land, though only a trifle more: indeed, the ship was so dangerously near that the heads of the Rakshasis with their widely-distended jaws almost touched its stern. The words which the Rakshasis uttered in the hearing of the crew and passengers were—"O sister, so

[1] A *yojana* is nearly eight miles.

you are going to eat them all yourself alone." The minister's son, the prefect's son, and the merchant's son had all along a suspicion that the pretended princess, the prince's partner, might after all also be a Rakshasi; that suspicion was now confirmed by what they heard the three Rakshasis say. Those words, however, produced no effect in the mind of the king's son, as from his intimate acquaintance with the princess he could not possibly take her to be a Rakshasi.

The captain told the four friends and princess that as he was bound for distant regions in search of gold mines, he could not take them along with him; he, therefore, proposed that on the next day he should put them ashore near some port, especially as they were now safe from the clutches of the Rakshasis. On the following day no port was visible for a long time; towards the evening, however, they came near a port where the four friends and the princess were landed. After walking some distance, the princess, who had never been accustomed to take long walks, complained of fatigue and hunger; they all therefore sat under a tree, and the king's son sent the merchant's son to buy some sweetmeats in the bazaar which they heard was not far off. The merchant's son did not return, as he was fully persuaded in his mind that the king's son's partner was as real a Rakshasi as the three others from whose clutches he had escaped. Seeing the delay of the merchant's son, the king's son sent the prefect's son after him; but neither did he return, he being also convinced that the pretended princess was a Rakshasi. The minister's son was next sent; but he also joined the other two. The king's son then himself went to the shop of the sweetmeat seller where he met his three friends, who made him remain with them by main force, earnestly declaring that the woman was no princess, but a real Rakshasi like the other three. Thus the princess was deserted by the four friends who returned to their own country, full of the adventures they had met with.

In the meantime the princess walked to the bazaar and found shelter for a few days in the house of a poor woman, after which she set out for the city of the four friends, the name and whereabouts of which city she had learnt from the king's son. On arriving at the city, she sold some of her costly ornaments, pearls and precious stones, and hired a stately house for her residence with a suitable establishment. She caused herself to be proclaimed as a heaven-born dice-player, and challenged all the players in the city to play, the conditions of the game being that if she lost it she would give the winner a *lakh*[1] of rupees, and if she won it she should get a *lakh* from him who lost the game. She also got authority from the king of the country to imprison in her own house any one who could not pay her the stipulated sum of money. The merchant's son, the prefect's son, and the minister's son, who all looked upon themselves as miraculous players, played with the princess, paid her many *lakhs*, but being unable to

[1] Ten thousand pounds sterling.

"Thus the princess was deserted."

WARWICK GOBLE

pay her all the sums they owed her, were imprisoned in her house. At last the king's son offered to play with her. The princess purposely allowed him to win the first game, which emboldened him to play many times, in all of which he was the loser; and being unable to pay the many *lakhs* owing her, the prince was about to be dragged into the dungeon, when the princess told him who she was. The merchant's son, the prefect's son, and the minister's son were brought out of their cells; and the joy of the four friends knew no bounds. The king and the queen received their daughter-in-law with open arms, and with demonstrations of great festivity.

Every one in the palace was glad except the princess. She could not forget that her parents, her brothers and sisters had been devoured by the Rakshasis, and that their bones, along with the bones of her father's subjects, stood in mountain heaps on the north side of the capital. The prince had told her that he and his three friends had the power of giving life to bones. They could then reconstruct the frames of her parents and other relatives; but the difficulty lay in this—how to kill the three Rakshasis. Could not the hermit, who taught them to give life, not teach also how to take away life? In all likelihood he could. Reasoning in this manner, the four friends and the princess went to the temple of the hermit in the forest, prayed to him to give them the secret of destroying life from a distance by a charm. The hermit became propitious, and granted the boon.

A deer was passing by at the moment. The hermit took a handful of water, repeated over it some words which the king's son distinctly heard, and threw it upon the deer. The deer died in a moment. He repeated other words over the dead animal, the deer jumped up and ran away into the forest.

Armed with this killing charm, the king's son, together with the princess and the three friends, went to his father-in-law's capital. As they approached the city of death, the three Rakshasis ran furiously towards them with open jaws. The king's son spilled charmed water upon them, and they died in an instant. They all then went to the heaps of bones. The merchant's son brought together the proper bones of the bodies, the prefect's son constructed them into skeletons, the minister's son clothed them with sinews, flesh, and skin, and the king's son gave them life. The princess was entranced at the sight of the re-animation of her parents and other relatives, and her eyes were filled with tears of joy. After a few days which they spent in great festivity, they left the revivified city, went to their own country, and lived many years in great happiness.

Here my story endeth,
The Natiya-thorn withereth, etc.

XXII

THE BALD WIFE

A CERTAIN man had two wives, the younger of whom he loved more than the elder. The younger wife had two tufts of hair on her head, and the elder only one. The man went to a distant town for merchandise; so the two wives lived together in the house. But they hated each other: the younger one, who was her husband's favourite, ill-treated the other. She made her do all the menial work in the house; rebuked her all day and night; and did not give her enough to eat. One day the younger wife said to the elder, "Come and take away all the lice from the hair of my head." While the elder wife was searching among the younger one's hair for the vermin, one lock of hair by chance gave way; on which the younger one, mightily incensed, tore off the single tuft that was on the head of the elder wife, and drove her away from the house. The elder wife, now become completely bald, determined to go into the forest, and there either die of starvation or be devoured by some wild beast. On her way she passed by a cotton plant. She stopped near it, made for herself a broom with some sticks which lay about, and swept clean the ground round about the plant. The plant was much pleased, and gave her a blessing. She wended on her way, and now saw a plantain tree. She swept the ground round about the plantain tree which, being pleased with her, gave her a blessing. As she went on she saw the shed of a Brahmani bull. As the shed was very dirty, she swept the place clean, on which the bull, being much pleased, blessed her. She next saw a *tulasi* plant, bowed herself down before it, and cleaned the place round about, on which the plant gave her a blessing. As she was going on in her journey she saw a hut made of branches of trees and leaves, and near it a man sitting cross-legged, apparently absorbed in meditation. She stood for a moment behind the venerable *muni*. "Whoever you may be," he said, "come before me; do not stand behind me; if you do, I will reduce you to ashes." The woman, trembling with fear, stood before the *muni*. "What is your petition?" asked the *muni*. "Father Muni," answered the woman, "thou knowest how miserable I am, since thou art all-knowing. My husband does not love me, and his other wife, having torn off the only tuft of hair on my head, has driven me away from the house. Have pity upon me, Father Muni!" The *muni*, continuing sitting, said, "Go into the tank which you see yonder. Plunge into the water only once, and then come to me again." The woman went to the tank, washed in it, and

WARWICK GOBLE

"When she got out of the water, what a change was seen in her!"

plunged into the water only once, according to the bidding of the *muni*. When she got out of the water, what a change was seen in her! Her head was full of jet black hair, which was so long that it touched her heels; her complexion had become perfectly fair; and she looked young and beautiful. Filled with joy and gratitude, she went to the *muni*, and bowed herself to the ground. The *muni* said to her, "Rise, woman. Go inside the hut, and you will find a number of wicker baskets, and bring out any you like." The woman went into the hut, and selected a modest-looking basket. The *muni* said, "Open the basket." She opened it, and found it filled with ingots of gold, pearls and all sorts of precious stones. The *muni* said, "Woman, take that basket with you. It will never get empty. When you take away the present contents their room will be supplied by another set, and that by another, and that by another, and the basket will never become empty. Daughter, go in peace." The woman bowed herself down to the ground in profound but silent gratitude, and went away.

As she was returning homewards with the basket in her hand, she passed by the *tulasi* plant whose bottom she had swept. The *tulasi* plant said to her, "Go in peace, child! thy husband will love thee warmly." She next came to the shed of the Brahmani bull, who gave her two shell ornaments which were twined round its horns, saying, "Daughter, take these shells, put them on your wrists, and whenever you shake either of them you will get whatever ornaments you wish to obtain." She then came to the plantain tree, which gave her one of its broad leaves, saying, "Take, child, this leaf; and when you move it you will get not only all sorts of delicious plantains, but all kinds of agreeable food." She came last of all to the cotton plant, which gave her one of its own branches, saying, "Daughter, take this branch; and when you shake it you will get not only all sorts of cotton clothes, but also of silk and purple. Shake it now in my presence." She shook the branch, and a fabric of the finest glossy silk fell on her lap. She put on that silk cloth, and wended on her way with the shells on her wrists, and the basket and the branch and the leaf in her hands.

The younger wife was standing at the door of her house, when she saw a beautiful woman approach her. She could scarcely believe her eyes. What a change! The old, bald hag turned into the very Queen of Beauty herself! The elder wife, now grown rich and beautiful, treated the younger wife with kindness. She gave her fine clothes, costly ornaments, and the richest viands. But all to no purpose. The younger wife envied the beauty and hair of her associate. Having heard that she got it all from Father Muni in the forest, she determined to go there. Accordingly she started on her journey. She saw the cotton plant, but did nothing to it; she passed by the plantain tree, the shed of the Brahmani bull, and the *tulasi* plant, without taking any notice of them. She approached the *muni.* The *muni* told her to bathe in the tank, and plunge only once into the water. She gave one plunge, at which she got a glorious head of hair and a beautifully fair complexion. She thought a second plunge would make her still more beautiful. Accordingly she plunged into the water again, and came out as bald and ugly as before. She came to the *muni*, and wept. The sage drove her away, saying, "Be off, you disobedient woman. You will get no boon from me." She went back to her house mad with grief. The lord of the two women returned from his travels and was struck with the long locks and beauty of his first wife. He loved her dearly ; and when he saw her secret and untold resources and her incredible wealth, he almost adored her. They lived together happily for many years, and had for their maid-servant the younger woman, who had been formerly his best beloved.

Here my story endeth,
The Natiya-thorn withereth ;
"*Why, O Natiya-thorn, dost wither ?*"
"*Why does thy cow on me browse ?*"
"*Why, O cow, dost thou browse ?*"
"*Why does thy neat-herd not tend me ?*"
"*Why, O neat-herd, dost not tend the cow ?*"
"*Why does thy daughter-in-law not give me rice ?*"
"*Why, O daughter-in-law, dost not give rice ?*"

"Why does my child cry?"
"Why, O child, dost thou cry?"
"Why does the ant bite me?"
"Why, O ant, dost thou bite?"
Koot! koot! koot!

THE END